Let Me
Count the Ways

✸ ✸ ✸

Let Me
Count the Ways

* * *

AN ANTHOLOGY OF LOVE

Fiona Castle

Hodder & Stoughton
LONDON   SYDNEY   AUCKLAND

British Library Cataloguing in Publication Data
A record for this book is available from
the British Library

ISBN 0340 78562 4

Printed and bound in Great Britain
by Clays Ltd, St Ives plc

Hodder and Stoughton
A Division of Hodder Headline Ltd
338 Euston Road
London NW1 3BH

Contents

❋ ❋ ❋

Acknowledgments

* * *

While every effort has been made to contact the copyright holders of material used in this book, this has not always been successful. Full acknowledgment will gladly be made in future editions.

We gratefully acknowledge the following, extracts from which appear in this book:

Eddie Askew, *Disguises of Love*, published by The Leprosy Mission International.

Alistair Begg, *The Hand of God*, Moody Press. Copyright © 1999. Used with permission.

Dietrick Bonhoeffer, *Life Together*, SCM Press, 1954.

Bob Gass, *The Word for Today*, published by United Christian Broadcasters and used by permission. For free issues of *The Word for Today*, contact UCB at Hanchurch Christian Centre, Stoke on Trent, ST4 8RY, www.ucb.co.uk

Ernest Gordon, *Miracle on the River Kwai*, HarperCollins Ltd.

Selwyn Hughes, *Reflections*, used by kind permission of the author.

Barbara Johnson, *Fresh Elastic for Stretched Out Mums*, HarperCollins Ltd.

Susan Lenzkes, *Crossing the Bridge Between You and Me*. Copyright © 1994 by Discovery House Publishers. All rights reserved.

C.S. Lewis, *Mere Christianity*. Copyright © C.S. Lewis Pte. Ltd. 1942, 1943, 1944, 1952. Extract reprinted by permission.

Living Light: Selections from the Living Bible, Kingsway, 1975. Used by permission of Kingsway Publications Ltd and Tyndale House Publishers.

Carole Mayhall, *Words that Hurt, Words that Heal*, 1986. Used by permission of NavPress Publishing (Colorado Springs, CO, USA).

Touchpoint Bible: God's Word at Your Point of Need (New Living Translation), Tyndale House Publishers, 1996. Used by permission of Tyndale House Publishers.

Michel Quoist, *Prayers of Life*, Gill & Macmillan Ltd.

John Powell, *Through the Seasons of the Heart*, HarperCollins Ltd.

Charles Ringma, *Dare to Journey*, used by kind permission of the author.

Helen Roseveare, *Living Faith*, Bethany House Publishers, 1980. Used by permission of WEC International.

Philip Yancey, *Where Is God When It Hurts?*, HarperCollins Ltd.

The following are also gratefully acknowledged:

Harry Boyle, 'Love Defined', used by kind permission of the author.

Johnny Burke and Jimmy Van Heusen, 'But Beautiful'. Words by Johnny Burke. Music by Jimmy Van Heusen. Copyright © 1947 by Burke & Van Heusen Inc., a division of Bourne Co., and

Dorsey Bros. Music copyright renewed. All rights reserved. International copyright secured.

Johnny Burke and Jimmy Van Heusen, 'Here's that Rainy Day'. Words by Johnny Burke. Music by Jimmy Van Heusen. Copyright © 1949 by Burke & Van Heusen Inc., a division of Bourne Co., and Dorsey Bros. Music copyright renewed. All rights reserved. International copyright secured.

Johnny Burke and Jimmy Van Heusen, 'So Would I'. Words by Johnny Burke. Music by Jimmy Van Heusen. Copyright © 1946 by Burke & Van Heusen Inc., a division of Bourne Co., and Dorsey Bros. Music copyright renewed. All rights reserved. International copyright secured.

Timothy Dudley-Smith, 'Lord, for the Years', copyright © 1967, used by kind permission of the author.

Graham Kendrick, 'My Lord, What Love Is This'. Used by permission of Make Way Music, PO Box 263, Croydon, Surrey, CR9 5AP, UK.

Graham Kendrick, 'Such Love'. Used by permission of Make Way Music, PO Box 263, Croydon, Surrey, CR9 5AP, UK.

Spike Milligan, 'Christmas 1959', used by kind permission of the author.

Spike Milligan, 'It Was Summer', used by kind permission of the author.

Nanette Newman, 'Lots of Love'. Copyright © Brian Forbes Ltd 2001.

Michael Palin, 'There Was a Tortoise Called Joe', taken from *Limericks* by Michael Palin and published by Red Fox. Used by permission of The Random House Group Ltd.

CHAPTER ONE

Love

✳ ✳ ✳

HOW DO I LOVE THEE?

How do I love thee? Let me count the ways.
I love thee to the depth and breadth and height
My soul can reach, when feeling out of sight
For the ends of Being and ideal Grace.
I love thee to the level of every day's
Most quiet need, by sun and candlelight.
I love thee freely, as men strive for Right;
I love thee purely, as they turn from Praise.
I love thee with the passion put to use
In my old griefs, and with my childhood's faith.
I love thee with a love I seemed to lose
With my lost saints, – I love thee with the breath,
Smiles, tears, of all my life! – and, if God choose,
I shall but love thee better after death.

Elizabeth Barrett Browning

*T*his beautiful love poem by Elizabeth Barrett Browning from her Sonnets from the Portuguese inspired the title of this 'anthology of love'. We tend to think of love as being a romantic, emotional feeling and yet there are so many different kinds of love. The Greek language is rich with a variety of words that express love whereas the English language is restricted to the one word 'love'. For instance, eros means romantic or erotic love, philia means brotherly love, and agape means self-giving, sacrificial love.

The Oxford Dictionary defines love as 'warm affection, attachment, liking or fondness, patience, benevolence and affectionate devotion'. Through the pages of this book I shall endeavour to 'count the ways' of love, to encourage, challenge, amuse and, above all, to emphasise that love is the 'better way'.

And now I will show you the most excellent way.

1 Corinthians 12:31 (NIV)

There are three things that will endure – faith, hope, and love – and the greatest of these is love.

1 Corinthians 13:13 (NLT)

LOVE DEFINED

Love, tender embrace,
An outreach of unfurled arms
Grasping in emotion.

Love basks in affection,
For someone, or some need,
A human desire.

Love dwells in pure kindness,
Spirit of offering –
Joy of giving.

Love nestles in friendship,
Goodwill of a handshake,
Warmth of a smile.

Love thrives in relationship,
Of family harmony,
Mother child affinity.

Love breathes understanding,
Comforting those in need,
Sharing and caring.

Love, mutual in togetherness,
Betrothed in life,
In sunshine, through shower.

Yet – love may be unknown.

Harry Boyle, An Anthology of Poetry, *sold in aid of Macmillan Cancer Relief and Queenscourt Hospices*

Love sought is good, but giv'n unsought is better.

William Shakespeare, Twelfth Night

Gracious Spirit, Holy Ghost,
Taught by Thee, we covet most
Of Thy gifts at Pentecost,
Holy, heavenly love.

Love is kind, and suffers long,
Love is meek, and thinks no wrong.
Love than death itself more strong;
Therefore give us love.

Prophecy will fade away,
Melting in the light of day;
Love will ever with us stay;
Therefore give us love.

Faith will vanish into sight;
Hope be emptied in delight;
Love in heaven will shine more bright;
Therefore give us love.

Faith and hope we love to see
Joining hand in hand agree;
But the greatest of the three,
And the best is love.

From the overshadowing
Of Thy gold and silver wing
Shed on us, who to Thee sing,
Holy, heavenly love.

Bishop Christopher Wordsworth

O ye who taste that love is sweet,
Set waymarks for all doubtful feet
That stumble on in search of it.

Sing notes of love: that some who hear
Far off, inert, may lend an ear,
Rise up and wonder and draw near.

Lead lives of love; that others who
Behold your life may kindle too
With love, and cast their lot with you.

Christina Rossetti

THE GIFT OF LOVE

Sustaining its Fragile Nature

Poets, philosophers and romantics have all sought to laud, describe and celebrate the mystery of love. In religious systems, love is usually described in terms of obedience and self-giving to the deity, while in psychological terms love has to do with caring relationships and a mutuality in which the boundaries of each person are respected.

No matter which way we approach the subject of love, our descriptions will only be haltingly inadequate. Henri Nouwen seeks to emphasise the vulnerability of love. He writes: 'In love men and women take off all the forms of power, embracing each other in total disarmament.'

Love will always have a fragile character. It cannot be regulated or sustained by structures, rules or commitments. It can only be sustained by continuing acts of love which are marked by gentleness, care, openness and trust.

Charles Ringma, Dare to Journey

It is not only necessary to love, it is necessary to say so.

French saying

Measure thy life by loss instead of gain,
Not by the wine drunk, but by the wine poured
    forth;
For love's strength standeth in love's sacrifice;
And he who suffers most has most to give.

Anon.

The way to love anything is to realise it might be lost.

G. K. Chesterton

We may, if we choose, make the worst of one another. Everyone has his weak points; everyone has his faults; we may make the worst of these. But we may also make the best of one another. We may forgive, even as we hope to be forgiven. We may put ourselves in the place of others, and ask what we should wish to be done to us, and thought of us, were we in their place. By loving whatever is loveable in those around

us, love will flow back from them to us, and
life will become a pleasure instead of a pain;
and earth will become like heaven; and we
shall become not unworthy followers of Him
whose name is Love.

Arthur Penryhn Stanley

Keep love in your heart,
A life without it
Is like a sunless garden …
The consciousness of loving and being loved
Brings a warmth
And richness to life
That nothing else can bring.

Oscar Wilde

CHAPTER TWO

God's Love for Us

❊ ❊ ❊

*P*robably the most important verse in the Bible is
John 3:16: 'For God so loved the world that he
gave his only Son so that everyone who believes in
him will not perish but have eternal life.' It is the truth
on which the whole of the Christian faith is based. It
tells of God's love for us to the extent that he sent his
Son Jesus – God of the Universe poured into a human
mould – to identify with us, in all our struggles here
on earth, dying an agonising death on the cross as a
once-and-for-all sacrifice for our sins. He did that, the
Bible tells us, in order that our relationship with him
might be restored. Jesus paid the price.

'God did not send his Son into the world to
condemn it, but to save it. There is no
judgment awaiting those who trust him. But
those who do not trust him have already
been judged for not believing in the only
Son of God.'

John 3:17–18 (NLT)

The phrase 'His own love' is very beautiful; it is God's own peculiar individual love, just as the love of a mother is her own peculiar love. Every different kind of love illustrates some aspect of God's love; but it must not be forgotten that the love of God is His own peculiar love.

Oswald Chambers

YOU LAID ASIDE YOUR MAJESTY

You laid aside your majesty,
Gave up everything for me,
Suffered at the hands of those You had created.
You took all my guilt and shame,
When you died and rose again;
Now today You reign,
In heaven and earth exalted.

I really want to worship You, my Lord,
You have won my heart
And I am yours for ever and ever;
I will love You.
You are the only one who died for me,
Gave Your life to set me free,
So I lift my voice to You in adoration.

Noel Richards

We are of such great value to God that he came to live among us ... and to guide us home. He will go to any length to seek us, even to being lifted high upon a cross to draw us back to himself. We can only respond by loving God for his love.

Catherine of Siena

LOVE

Love bade me welcome; yet my soul drew back,
Guilty of dust and sin.
But quick-eyed Love, observing me grow slack
From my first entrance in,
Drew nearer to me, sweetly questioning
If I lacked anything.

'A guest,' I answered, 'Worthy to be here.'
Love said, 'You shall be he.'
'I, the unkind, ungrateful? Ah, my dear,
I cannot look on thee.'
Love took my hand and smiling did reply,
'Who made the eyes but I?'

'Truth, Lord, but I have marred them: let my
    shame
Go where it doth deserve.'
'And know you not,' says Love, 'Who bore
    the blame?'
'My dear, then I will serve.'
'You must sit down,' says Love, 'and taste my
    meat.'
So I did sit and eat.

George Herbert

The Christian is in a different position from
other people who are trying to be good.
They hope, by being good, to please God if
there is one; or – if they think there is not –
at least they hope to deserve approval; from
good men. But the Christian thinks any
good he does comes from the Christ-life
inside him. He does not think God will love
us because we are good, but that God will
make us good because He loves us.

C. S. Lewis

22

'Let the children come to me. Don't stop them! For the Kingdom of God belongs to such as these. I assure you, anyone who doesn't have their kind of faith will never get into the Kingdom of God.'

Mark 10:14–15 (NLT)

The following is one of the best-known children's hymns, which I remember very well from my childhood. Adults might find the words simplistic and yet Jesus calls us to have a childlike faith. How he loved the forthrightness of children!

It is a thing most wonderful,
Almost too wonderful to be,
That God's own Son should come from heaven.
And die to save a child like me.

And yet I know that it is true:
He chose a poor and humble lot,
And wept and toiled and mourned and died
For love of those who loved Him not.

I cannot tell how He could love
A child so weak and full of sin;
His love must be most wonderful,
If He could die my love to win.

I sometimes think about the cross,
And shut my eyes and try to see
The cruel nails and crown of thorns,
And Jesus crucified for me.

But even could I see Him die,
I could but see a little part
Of that great love which, like a fire,
Is always burning in His heart.

It is most wonderful to know
His love for me so free and sure;
But 'tis more wonderful to see
My love for Him so faint and poor.

And yet, I want to love Thee, Lord!
O light the flame within my heart,
And I will love Thee more and more,
Until I see Thee as Thou art.

Bishop W. Walsham How

GOD'S LOVE OF MAN

God loves you. You're rebellious, you cheat, you commit immorality, you're selfish, you sin, but God loves you with an intensity beyond anything that I could describe to you. He loves you, and He loves you so much that He gave His only Son, Jesus Christ to die on the cross; and the thing that kept Christ on that cross was love, not the nail.

Billy Graham

I have really appreciated the writings and poetry of Eddie Askew in the books he has written to benefit the Leprosy Mission. He expresses so beautifully what many of us feel and yet fail to put into words adequately. Thank you, Eddie.

Lord, I realise that what I see of your love
Is only the beginning
One drop from the whole ocean.
Sand, like the sea, moving, surging.
All embracing.

Seeking to surround me,
Not to overwhelm, to drown,
But to hold me, buoy me up.
A love with room to spare.
No rejections.
No high-tide mark of rubbish,
Pushed up and thrown aside

I wish Judas could have known that.
I wish that somehow
In his own agony in the garden,
So different, Lord, from yours,
So like mine,
He could have reached out
From the depths of his despair
And felt your hand.
There's nothing I can do about that.
I leave it with you, Lord,
As I leave so much, You've got strong hands.

But one thing, Lord,
Judas stays in my thoughts
And, in a strange way,
Comforts me.
Because I know beyond doubt
That when I'm nearly overwhelmed
In my own betrayals,
It isn't you who puts space between us.
It's me.
You are still there,
With your forgiveness, As you forgave Peter,
And Thomas, and Paul,
So you forgive me.

And accept me, as you accepted them.
Thank you seems so small a word,
But it's all I've got.

Eddie Askew, The Disguises of Love

This hymn is one of the most popular wedding
hymns, probably chosen because most people
know the tune and it talks about love. How sad that
many would sing it missing the truth of the words ...
that God's love for us surpasses all forms of human
love and that love is waiting and longing to enter
every human heart.

Love divine, all loves excelling,
Joy of heav'n to earth come down!
Fix in us thy humble dwelling,
All Thy faithful mercies crown.
Jesu, thou art all compassion,
Pure unbounded love thou art;
Visit us with thy salvation,
Enter every trembling heart.

Breathe, O breathe thy loving Spirit
Into every troubled breast!
Let us all in thee inherit,
Let us find thy promised rest.
Take away the love of sinning;
Alpha and Omega be;
End of faith, as its beginning,
Set our hearts at liberty.

Come, almighty to deliver,
Let us all thy grace receive!
Suddenly return, and never,
Never more thy temples leave.
Thee we would be always blessing,
Serve thee as thy hosts above,
Pray, and praise thee without ceasing,
Glory in thy perfect love.

Finish then thy new creation,
Pure and spotless let us be;
Let us see thy great salvation
Perfectly restored in thee!
Changed from glory into glory,
Till in heaven we take our place;
Till we cast our crowns before thee,
Lost in wonder, love and praise.

Charles Wesley

I will be your God throughout your lifetime
– until your hair is white with age. I made
you, and will care for you. I will carry you
along and save you.

Isaiah 46:4 (NLT)

Here is love, that God sent His Son. His Son who never offended. His Son who was always His delight. Herein is love, that He sent Him to save sinners; to save them by bearing their sins, by bearing their curse, by dying their death, and by carrying their sorrows.

Here is love, in that while we were yet enemies, Christ died for us; yes, here is love, in that while we were yet without strength, Christ died for the ungodly.

John Bunyan

SUCH LOVE

Such love, pure as the whitest snow,
Such love, weeps for the shame I know,
Such love, paying the debt I owe,
O Jesus, such love.

Such love, stilling my restlessness,
Such love, filling my emptiness,
Such love, showing me holiness,
O Jesus, such love.

Such love, springs from eternity,
Such love, streaming through history,
Such love, fountain of life to me,
O Jesus, such love.

Graham Kendrick

*T*he following anecdote was sent to me about a WEC missionary, Dr Helen Roseveare. I had the privilege of hearing her tell her story of her time in the Congo (now Zaire) where many of her fellow missionaries were murdered. A statement she made astounded me at the time and has remained with me to help and encourage me on so many occasions: 'God saves some people from death and others He saves through death.'

A LITTLE GIRL'S PRAYER

One night I had worked hard to help a mother in the labour ward; but in spite of all we could do she died leaving us with a tiny premature baby and a crying two-year-old daughter. We would have difficulty keeping the baby alive, as we had no incubator (we had no electricity to run an incubator) and no special feeding facilities.

Although we lived on the equator, nights were often chilly with treacherous draughts. One student midwife went for the box we had for such babies and the cotton wool the baby would be wrapped in. Another went to stoke up the fire and fill a hot water bottle. She came back shortly in distress to tell me that in filling the bottle it had burst. Rubber perishes easily in tropical climates. 'And it is our last hot water bottle!' she exclaimed.

As in the West, it is no good crying over spilt milk, so in Central Africa it might be considered no good crying over burst water bottles. They do not grow on trees, and there are no drugstores down forest pathways.

'All right,' I said. 'Put the baby as near the fire as you safely can; sleep between the baby and the door to keep it free from draughts. Your job is to keep the baby warm.'

The following noon, as I did most days, I went to have prayers with any of the orphanage children who chose to gather with me. I gave the youngsters various suggestions of things to pray about and told them about the tiny baby. I explained our problem about keeping the baby warm enough, mentioning the hot water bottle. The baby could so easily die if it got chills. I also told them of the two-year-old sister, crying because her mother had died.

During the prayer time, one ten-year-old girl, Ruth, prayed with the usual blunt conciseness of our African children. 'Please, God,' she prayed, 'send us a water bottle. It'll be no good tomorrow, God, as the baby'll be dead, so please send it this afternoon.' While I gasped inwardly at the audacity of the prayer, she added, by way of corollary, 'And while you are about it, would You please send a dolly for the little girl so she'll know You really love her.'

As often with children's prayers, I was put on the spot. Could I honestly say 'Amen'? I just did not believe that God could do this.

Oh, yes, I know that God can do everything. The Bible says so. But there are limits, aren't there? The only way God could answer this particular prayer would be by sending me a parcel from the homeland. I had been in Africa almost four years at that time, and I never, ever received a parcel from home. Anyway, if anyone did send me a parcel, who would put in a hot water bottle? I lived on the equator!

Halfway through the afternoon, while I was teaching in the nurses' training school, a message was sent that there was a car at my front door. By the time I reached home, the car had gone, but there, on the veranda, was a large twenty-two pound parcel! I felt tears pricking my eyes. I could not open the parcel alone, so I sent for the orphanage children. Together we pulled off the string, carefully undoing each knot. We folded the paper, taking care not to tear it unduly.

Excitement was mounting. Some thirty or forty pairs of eyes were focussed on the large cardboard box.

From the top, I lifted out brightly coloured, knitted jerseys. Eyes sparkled as I gave them out. There were the knitted bandages for the leprous patients, and the children looked a little bored. Then came a box of mixed raisins and sultanas – that would make a nice batch of buns for the weekend. Then, as I put my hand in again, I felt the ... could it really be? I grasped it and pulled it out – yes! A brand new rubber hot water bottle! I cried. I had not asked God to send it, I had not truly believed that He could.

Ruth was in the front row of the children. She rushed forward, crying out, 'If God has sent the hot water bottle, He must have sent the dolly, too!'

Rummaging down to the bottom of the box, she pulled out the small, beautifully dressed dolly. Her eyes shone! She had never doubted!

Looking up at me she asked, 'Can I go over with you, Mummy, and give this dolly to that little girl, so she'll know that Jesus really loves her?'

That parcel had been on the way for five whole months! Packed up by my former Sunday school class, whose leader had heard and obeyed God's prompting to send a hot water bottle, even to the equator. And one of the girls had put in a dolly for an African child – five months before, in answer to the believing prayer of a ten-year-old to bring it 'that afternoon'.

'Before they call, I will answer!' (Isaiah 65:24).

Helen Roseveare

Add to your brotherliness ... love.

2 Peter 1:7

Love is indefinite to most of us, we do not know what we mean when we talk about love. Love is the sovereign preference of one person for another, and spiritually Jesus demands that the preference be for Himself (cf. Luke 14:26). When the love of God is shed abroad in our hearts by the Holy Ghost, Jesus Christ is easily first; then we must practise the working out of these things mentioned by Peter.

The first thing God does is to knock pretence and the pious pose right out of me. The Holy Spirit reveals that God loved me not because I was loveable, but because it was His nature to do so. 'Now,' He says to me, 'show the same love to others – *Love as I have loved you*. I will bring any number of people about you whom you cannot respect, and you must exhibit my love to them as I have exhibited it to you. *You won't reach it on tiptoe*'. Some of us have tried, but we were soon tired.

'The Lord suffereth long ...' Let me look within and see His dealings with me. The knowledge that God has loved me to the uttermost, to the end of all my meanness and selfishness and wrong, will send me forth into the world to love in the same way.

God's love to me is inexhaustible, and I must love others from the bedrock of God's love to me. Growth in grace stops the moment I get huffed. I get huffed because I have a peculiar person to live with. Just think how disagreeable I have been to God! Am I prepared to be so identified with the Lord Jesus that His life and His sweetness are being poured out all the time? Neither natural love nor Divine love will remain unless it is cultivated. Love is spontaneous, but it has to be maintained by discipline.

Oswald Chambers, My Utmost for His Highest

Many of the hymns and poems I have chosen were written centuries ago. However, there is continuity through the ages of God's unchanging love for us. Though fashions change, technology advances at an amazing rate, human emotions, problems and sufferings and God's answer to them remain the same.

Seek his will in all you do, and he will direct your paths.

Proverbs 3:6 (NLT)

'In pastures green?' Not always; sometimes He
Who knows best, in kindness leadeth me
In weary ways, where heavy shadows be.

So, whether on the hill-tops high and fair
I dwell, or in the sunless valleys, where
The shadows lie, what matter? He is there.

Henry H. Hardy

The Shepherd knows what pastures are best
for His sheep, and they must not question
nor doubt, but trustingly follow Him.
Perhaps He sees that the best pastures for
some of us are to be found in the midst of
opposition or of earthly trials. If He leads
you there, you may be sure they are green
for you, and you will grow and be made
strong by feeding there. Perhaps He sees
that the best waters for you to walk beside
will be raging waves of trouble and sorrow.
If this should be the case, He will make
them still waters for you, and you must go
and lie down beside them, and let them have
their blessed influences on you.

Anon., taken from Daily Strength for Daily Needs

The Lord is good. When trouble comes He is a strong refuge. And He knows everyone who trusts in Him.

Nahum 1:7 (NLT)

GREAT AND WRETCHED

Consider Jesus Christ in every person, and in ourselves, Jesus Christ as father in his father, Jesus Christ as brother in his brothers, Jesus Christ as poor in the poor, Jesus Christ as rich in the rich, Jesus Christ as priest and doctor in priests. Jesus Christ as sovereign in princes. For by his glory he is everything that is great, being God, and by his mortal life he is everything that is wretched and abject. That is why he took on this unhappy condition, so that he could be in every person and a model for every condition of men.

Blaise Pascal

For His great love has compassed
Our nature, and our need.
We know not; but He knoweth,
And He will bless indeed.
Therefore, O heavenly Father,
Give what is best to me;
And take the things unanswered,
As offerings made to Thee.

Anon.

A friend once sent this to me to encourage me!

You: It's impossible.
God: All things are possible. (*Luke 18:27*)

You: I'm too tired.
God: I will give you rest. (*Matthew 11:28-30*)

You: Nobody really loves me.
God: I love you. (*John 3:16; 13:34*)

You: I can't go on.
God: My grace is sufficient. (*2 Corinthians 12:9; Psalm 91:15*)

You: I can't figure things out.
God: I will direct your steps. (*Proverbs 3:5-6*)

You: I can't do it.
God: You can do all things. (*Philippians 4:13*)

You: I'm not able.
God: I am able. (*2 Corinthians 9:8*)

You: It's not worth it.
God: It will be worth it. (*Romans 8:28*)

You: I can't forgive myself.
God: I FORGIVE YOU. (*1 John 1:9;
    Romans 8:1*)

You: I can't manage.
God: I will supply all your needs.
    (*Philippians 4:19*)

You: I'm afraid.
God: I have not given you a spirit of fear.
    (*2 Timothy 1:17*)

You: I'm always worried and frustrated.
God: Cast all your cares on ME. (*1 Peter
    5:7*)

You: I don't have enough faith.
God: I've given everyone a measure of faith.
    (*Romans 12:3*)

You: I'm not smart enough.
God: I give you wisdom. (*1 Corinthians 1:30*)

You: I feel all alone.

God: I will never leave you or forsake you.
(*Hebrews 13:50*)

*H*ere is one of my favourite passages in the Bible.

PAUL'S PRAYER FOR SPIRITUAL EMPOWERING

When I think of the wisdom and scope of God's plan, I fall to my knees and pray to the Father, the Creator of everything in heaven and on earth. I pray that from his glorious, unlimited resources he will give you mighty inner strength through his Holy Spirit. And I pray that Christ will be more and more at home in your hearts as you trust in him. May your roots go deep down into the soil of God's marvellous love. And may you have the power to understand, as all God's people should, how wide, how long, how high, and how deep his love really is. May you experience the love of Christ, though it is so great you will never fully understand it. Then you will be filled with the fullness of life and power that comes from God.

Ephesians 3:14–19 (NLT)

SECURITY

Ephesians 3:14-21

This passage is like a great reassuring love note from God. We are reminded that, as believers, we have received the resources and inner strength of Christ Himself, Who lives in our hearts through the Holy Spirit.

We are also given a marvellous illustration of how inexhaustible God's love for us is. God's love is wide enough to cover all of us, long enough to last into eternity, high enough to include our moments of greatest joy and triumph, and deep enough to sustain us through our most overwhelming discouragement.

When we feel insecure, it seems that some crucial part of us is missing. When you feel that inner longing, remember that God's overwhelming love takes us beyond our deepest need or greatest hope.

Touchpoint – New Living Translation Bible

When I first became a Christian my sister Liza, gave me a tiny book called The Practice of the Presence of God *– conversations with Brother Lawrence of the Carmelite community in Paris in 1666. They are an amazing record of the thoughts and faith of this most humble man who was converted at the age of eighteen. Here is an extract.*

God knoweth best what is needful for us, and all that He does is for our good. If we knew how much He loves us, we should be always ready to receive equally and with indifference from His hand the sweet and the bitter; all would please that came from Him. The sorest afflictions never appear intolerable but when we see them in the wrong light: when we see them in the hand of God, Who dispenses them; we know that it is our loving Father, Who abases and distresses us; our sufferings will lose their bitterness, and become even matter of consolation.

Let all our employment be to know God: the more one knows Him, the more one desires to know Him. And as knowledge is commonly the measure of love, the deeper and more extensive our knowledge shall be the greater will be our love: and if our love of God were great we should love Him equally in pains and pleasures. Let us not amuse ourselves to seek to love God for any sensible favours (how elevated soever) which He has or may do us. Such favours, though never so great cannot bring us so near to God as faith does in one simple act. Let us seek Him often by faith: He is within us; seek Him not elsewhere. Are we not rude and deserve blame, if we leave Him alone to busy ourselves with trifles, which do not please Him, and perhaps offend Him? 'Tis to be feared these trifles will one day cost us dear.

Let us begin to be devoted to Him in good earnest. Let us cast everything besides out of our hearts; He would possess them alone.

God's love for me is inexhaustible, and His love for me is the basis of my love for others. We have to love where we cannot respect and where we must not respect, and this can only be done on the basis of God's love for us. 'This is My commandment, that ye love one another, as I have loved you.'

Oswald Chambers

CHAPTER THREE

Our Love for God

* * *

ON LOVE OF GOD

'Thou shalt love the Lord thy God with thy whole heart, with thy whole soul and with thy whole mind.' This is the commandment of the great God, and He cannot command the impossible. Love is a fruit in season at all times, and within reach of every hand. Anyone may gather it and no limit is set.

Mother Teresa

My Jesus, I love Thee, I know Thou art mine;
For Thee all the pleasures of sin I resign.
My gracious Redeemer, my Saviour art Thou;
If ever I loved Thee, my Jesus, 'tis now.

I love Thee because Thou has first lov'd me
And purchased my pardon on Calvary's tree.
I love Thee for wearing the thorns on Thy brow;
If ever I loved Thee, my Jesus, 'tis now.

In mansions of glory and endless delight
I'll ever adore Thee in heaven so bright.
I'll sing with a glittering crown on my brow,
If ever I loved Thee, my Jesus, 'tis now.

William R. Featherston/Adoniram J. Gordon

The majority of us have an ethereal,
unpractical, bloodless abstraction which we
call 'love for God'; to Jesus love for God
meant the most passionate intense love of
which a human being is capable.

Oswald Chambers

We love because he first loved us.

1 John 4:19 (NIV)

This beautiful song by Matt Redman expresses the love of our hearts when we discover who Jesus is and what he has done for us.

I WILL OFFER UP MY LIFE

I will offer up my life
In spirit and truth,
Pouring out the oil of love
As my worship to you.
In surrender I must give
My every part.
Lord, receive the sacrifice
Of a broken heart.

You deserve my every breath,
For you've paid the great cost –
Giving up your life to death,
Even death on a cross.
You took all my shame away,
There defeated my sin,
Opened up the gates of heaven
And have beckoned me in.

Jesus, what can I give,
What can I bring?
To so faithful a friend,
To so loving a king?
Saviour, what can be said,
What can be sung
as a praise of your Name
for the things you have done?
Oh, my words cannot tell,
Not even in part,
Of the debt of love that is owed
By this thankful heart.

Matt Redman

ABOUND IN YOU

Sever me from myself that I may be grateful to you;
may I perish to myself that I may be safe in you;
may I die to myself that I may live in you;
may I wither to myself that I may blossom in you;
may I be emptied of myself that I may abound in
    you;
may I be nothing to myself that I may be all to you.

Desiderius Erasmus

*T*he following paragraph is from Reflections, a book by Selwyn Hughes, who has provided me and millions of others with daily Bible teaching through his notes Every Day with Jesus, which he has faithfully and inspiringly produced for thirty-five years.

LOVEST THOU *ME*?

When Jesus Christ was about to leave this world He placed His affairs largely in the hands of one man – Simon Peter (John 21:15–17). Now, as you may admit, that appeared a very daring thing to do, especially as Peter had not proved too trustworthy in the past. Yet Jesus did not hesitate to do it.

Before handing to him the tremendous responsibility of holding the keys of the kingdom, however, there was something about which Jesus wanted to be sure, and so taking Simon Peter aside He asked him a thrice-repeated question. What was it? 'Peter, are you familiar with the principles of public speaking?' No. 'Peter, do you understand the technical details of my religion?' No. 'Peter, are you able to handle the financial matters relating to My Church?' No. What was it then? IT was this: 'Peter, do you love Me?' And that, brothers and sisters, is the core of Christianity.

Selwyn Hughes

My love is deep,
The more I give to thee
The more I have,
For both are infinite.

William Shakespeare

Take my life, and let it be
Consecrated, Lord, to Thee;
Take my moments and my days,
Let them flow in ceaseless praise.

Take my hands, and let them move
At the impulse of Thy love;
Take my feet and let them be
Swift and beautiful for Thee.

Take my voice, and let me sing
Always, only, for my King;
Take my lips, and let them be
Filled with messages from Thee.

Take my silver and my gold,
Not a mite would I withhold;
Take my intellect, and use
Every power as Thou shalt choose.

Take my will, and make it Thine;
It shall be no longer mine:
Take my heart, it is Thine own;
It shall be Thy royal throne.

Take my Love; my Lord, I pour
At Thy feet its treasure store:
Take myself, and I will be
Ever, only, all for Thee.

Francis Ridley Havergal

*O*ne of my favourite gospel singers is Larnelle
Harris. I love to listen to him in my car during
seemingly endless trips on the motorways, and to
lift my spirits, sing along too!

SEEKERS OF YOUR HEART

Until we give you first place
Until we let you begin
To fill us with your Spirit,
Renew us from within.
Nothing matters,
Nothing's gained,
Without your holy presence
Our lives are lived in vain.

Chorus
Lord, we want to know you,
Live our lives to show you
All the love we owe you.
We're seekers of your heart.

Because your heart was broken,
Because you saw the need,
Because you gave so freely,
Because of Calvary,
We can now be
Called your own,
Completed creations,
Filled with you alone.

Larnelle Harris

*M*any people who plan to meet God at the eleventh hour, die at ten thirty!

If human love does not carry a man beyond himself, it is not love. If love is always discreet, always wise, always sensible, and calculating, never carried beyond itself, it is not love at all. It may be affection, it may be warmth of feeling, but it has not the true nature of love in it.

Have I ever been carried away to do something for God not because it was my duty, nor because it was useful, nor because there was anything in it at all beyond the fact that I love Him? Have I ever realised that I can bring to God things which are of value to Him, or am I mooning round the magnitude of His Redemption whilst there are any number of things I might be doing?

Not Divine, colossal things which could be recorded as marvellous, but ordinary, simple human things which will give evidence to God that I am abandoned to Him? Have I ever produced in the heart of the Lord Jesus what Mary of Bethany produced?

There are times when it seems as if God watches to see if we will give Him the abandoned tokens of how genuinely we do love Him. Abandon to God is of more value than personal holiness. Personal holiness focuses the eye on our own whiteness; we are greatly concerned about the way we walk and talk and look, fearful lest we offend Him. Perfect love casts out all that, when once we are abandoned to God. We have to get rid of this notion – 'Am I of any use?' and make up our minds that we are not, and we may be near the truth. It is never a question of being of use, but of being of value to God Himself. When we are abandoned to God, He works through us all the time.

Oswald Chambers

NOTHING CAN SEPARATE US
FROM GOD'S LOVE

What can we say about such wonderful things as these? If God is for us, who can ever be against us? Since God did not spare even his own Son but gave him up for us all, won't God, who gave us Christ, also give us everything else?

Who dares accuse us whom God has chosen for his own? Will God? No! He is the one who has given us right standing with himself. Who then will condemn us? Will Christ Jesus? No, for he is the one who died for us and was raised to life for us and is sitting at the place of highest honour next to God, pleading for us.

Can anything ever separate us from Christ's love? Does it mean he no longer loves us if we have trouble or calamity, or are persecuted, or are hungry or cold or in danger or threatened with death? (Even the Scripture says, 'For your sake we are killed every day; we are being slaughtered like sheep.') No, despite all these things overwhelming victory is ours through Christ, who loved us.

And I am convinced that nothing can ever separate us from his love. Death can't, and life can't. The angels can't, and the demons can't. Our fears for today, our worries about tomorrow, and even the powers of hell can't keep God's love away. Whether we are high above the sky or in the deepest ocean,

nothing in all creation will ever be able to
separate us from the love of God that is
revealed in Christ Jesus our Lord.

Romans 8:31–39 (NLT)

Love of self is a stolen love
It was destined for others, they needed it to
    live, to thrive, and I have diverted it
So the love of self creates human suffering
So the love of men for themselves creates
    human misery
All the miseries of men, all the sufferings of
    men
The suffering of the boy whose mother has
    slapped him without cause, and that of the
    man whose boss has reprimanded him in
    front of the other workers
The suffering of the ugly girl neglected at a
    dance, and that of the woman whose
    husband doesn't kiss her anymore
The suffering of the child left at home because
    he's a nuisance, and that of the grandfather
    made fun of because he's too old
The suffering of the worried man who hasn't
    been able to confide in anyone, and that of
    the troubled adolescent whose worries have
    been ridiculed
The suffering of the separated man who jumps
    into the canal, and that of the criminal who
    is going to be executed

The suffering of the unemployed man who
wants to work, and that of the worker who
ruins his health for a ridiculous wage

The suffering of the father who has to pile his
family into a single room next to an empty
house, and that of the mother whose
children are hungry while the remains of
someone's party are thrown into the
dustbin

The suffering of one who dies alone while his
family, in the adjoining room, wait for his
death, drinking coffee

All sufferings

All injustices, bitternesses, humiliations, griefs,
hates, despairs,

All sufferings are an unappeased hunger

A hunger for love

So men have built, slowly, selfishness by
selfishness, a disfigured world that crushes
them

So men on earth spend their time feeding their
self-love. While around them others with
outstretched arms die of hunger

They have squandered love

I have squandered Your Love, Lord

Michel Quoist

CHAPTER FOUR

Romantic Love

* * *

SUMMER

It was summer –
    on the lake hung a golden haze,
It was summer –
    it was one of those endless days,
So we walked thru' a field of clover
    and then over
    a sheep-spun hill
And it seemed it would last for ever
      and it did – until
Came the evening,
    we swung on a garden gate,
It was heaven,
    you were seven and I was eight.
And we watched at the stars suspended,
Walking home down an apple lane,
Me and Rosie, a doll, a daisy chain,
On an evening that would never come again.

Spike Milligan

I suppose there are more poems and songs composed about romantic love than anything else! So many hopes and dreams are built into the ideal of love and 'happy ever after'. And it hasn't changed through the ages.

Probably the most famous love story of all time is Romeo and Juliet. *Here are two speeches that many of us will have memorised in our youth!*

ROMEO

But, soft! what light through yonder window
    breaks?
It is the east, and Juliet is the sun.
Arise, fair sun, and kill the envious moon,
Who is already sick and pale with grief
That thou her maid art far more fair than she.
Be not her maid, since she is envious;
Her vestal livery is but sick and green,
And none but fools do wear it: cast it off.
It is my lady; O, it is my love!
O that she knew she were!
She speaks, yet she says nothing: What of that?
Her eye discourses, I will answer it.
I am too bold, 'tis not to me she speaks:
Two of the fairest stars in all the heaven,
Having some business, do entreat her eyes
To twinkle in their spheres 'til they return.
What if her eyes were there, they in her head?
The brightness of her cheek would shame those
    stars,

As daylight doth a lamp; her eyes in heaven
Would through the airy region stream so bright
That birds would sing, and think it were not
      night.
See! how she leans her cheek upon her hand:
O! that I were a glove upon that hand,
That I might touch that cheek.

JULIET

Gallop apace, you fiery footed steeds,
Towards Phoebus' lodging; such a waggoner
As Phaethon would whip you to the west,
And bring the cloudy night immediately.
Spread thy close curtain, love-performing night!
That runaways' eyes may wink, and Romeo
Leap to these arms, untalked of and unseen!
Lovers can see to do their amorous rites
By their own beauties; or, if love be blind,
It best agrees with night. Come, civil night,
Thou sober-suited matron, all in black,
And learn me how to lose a winning match.
Played for a pair of stainless maidenhoods;
Hood my unmanned blood, bating in my cheeks,
With thy black mantle, till strange love, grown bold,
Think true love acted simple modesty.
Come night; come Romeo, come thou day in
      night,
For thou wilt lie upon the wings of night
Whiter than new snow upon a raven's back.
Come, gentle night; come, loving black-brow'd
      night,

Give me my Romeo: and, when he shall die,
Take him and cut him out in little stars,
And he will make the face of heaven so fine
That all the world will be in love with night,
And pay no worship to the garish sun.
O, I have bought the mansion of a love,
But not possessed it; and though I am sold,
Not yet enjoyed. So tedious is this day
As is the night before some festival
To an impatient child that hath new robes,
And may not wear them.

William Shakespeare, Romeo and Juliet

I remember the actress Virginia McKenna saying this poem in Lewis Gilbert's powerful film Carve Her Name with Pride, *which portrays the life of Violette Szabo.*

The life that I have
Is all that I have
And the life that I have
Is yours.

The love that I have
Of the life that I have
Is yours, and yours and yours.

A sleep I shall have,
A rest I shall have,
Yet death will be but a pause.

For the peace of my years
In the long green grass
Will be yours, and yours and yours.

Written for Violette Szabo

*C*armen McRae was a favourite singer of mine
during the late 1950s and early 1960s. This one
is but beautiful!

BUT BEAUTIFUL

Love is funny or it's sad
Or it's quiet or it's mad,
It's a good thing or it's bad –
But beautiful.

Beautiful to take a chance
And if you fall you fall
And I'm thinking I wouldn't mind at all
Love is tearful or it's gay
It's a problem or it's play
It's heartache either way –
But beautiful.

And I'm thinking if you were mine
I'd never let you go
And that would be but beautiful
I know.

Jimmy Van Heusen/Johnny Burke

The heart has its reasons which reason knows nothing of.

Blaise Pascal

*H*ere is a selection of classic love poems from past centuries.

A BIRTHDAY

My heart is like a singing bird
Whose nest is in a watered shoot;
My heart is like an apple tree
Whose bows are bent with thick-set fruit;
My heart is like a rainbow shell
That paddles in a halcyon sea;
My heart is gladder than all these
Because my love is come to me.

Raise me a dais of silk and down.
Hang it with vair and purple dyes;
Carve it in doves and pomegranates,
And peacocks with a hundred eyes.
Work it in gold and silver grapes,
In leaves and silver fleurs-de-lys;
Because the birthday of my life
Is come, my love is come to me.

Christina Rossetti

Thanks to the human heart by which we live,
Thanks to its tenderness, its joys, and fears,
To me the meanest flower that blows can give
Thoughts that do often lie too deep for tears.

William Wordsworth

SHE WALKS IN BEAUTY

She walks in beauty, like the night
Of cloudless climes and starry skies;
And all that's best of dark and bright
Meet in her aspect and her eyes:
Thus mellow'd to that tender light
Which heaven to gaudy day denies.

One shade the more, one ray the less
Had half impaired the nameless grace
Which waves in every raven tress,
Or softly lightens o'er her face;
Where thoughts serenely sweet express
How pure, how dear their dwelling-place.

And on that cheek, and o'er that brow,
So soft, so calm, yet eloquent,
The smiles that win, the tints that glow,
But tell of days in goodness spent,
A mind at peace with all below,
A heart whose love is innocent!

Lord Byron

If thou must love me, let it be for nought
Except for love's sake only. Do not say
'I love her for her smile – her look – her way
Of speaking gently – for a trick of thought
That falls in well with mine, and certes
    brought
A sense of pleasant ease on such a day' –
For these things in themselves, Beloved, may
Be changed, or change for thee – and love, so
    wrought
May be unwrought so. Neither love me for
Thine own dear pity's wiping my cheeks dry –
A creature might forget to weep, who bore
Thy comfort long, and lose thy love thereby!
But love me for love's sake, that evermore
Thou may'st love on, through love's eternity.

Elizabeth Barrett Browning

LOVE'S RIDDLE

'Unriddle this riddle, my own Jenny love,
Unriddle this riddle to me;
And if ye unriddle the riddles aright
A kiss your prize shall be,
And if ye riddle the riddles all wrong
Ye're treble the debt to me.

'I'll give thee an apple without any core,
I'll give thee a cherry where stones never be,
I'll give thee a palace without any door,
And thou shalt unlock it without any key.
I'll give thee a fortune that kings cannot give,
Nor anyone take it from thee.'

'How can there be apples without any core?
How can there be cherries where stones never
        be?
How can there be houses without any door
Or doors I may open without any key?
How canst thou give fortunes that kings
        cannot give
When thou art no richer than me?'

'My head is the apple without any core;
In cherries in blossom no stones never be;
My mind is love's palace without any door
Which thou canst unlock, love, without any
        key;
My heart is the wealth, love, that kings cannot
        give
Nor anyone take it from thee.

'So these are love's riddles, my own Jenny
      love,
Ye cannot unriddle to me;
And as for the one kiss ye've so easily lost
I'll make ye give seven to me.
To kiss thee is sweet, but 'tis sweeter by far
To be kissed, my dear Jenny, by thee.

'Come pay me the forfeit, my own Jenny love,
Thy kisses and cheeks are akin;
And for thy three sweet ones, I'll give thee a
      score
On thy cheeks and thy lips and thy chin.'
She laughed while he gave them, and much as
      to say
'Twere better to lose than to win.

John Clare

SONNET 18

Shall I compare thee to a summer's day?
Thou art more lovely and more temperate:
Rough winds do shake the darling buds of May,
And summer's lease hath all too short a date:
Sometimes too hot the eye of heaven shines,
And often is his gold complexion dimmed;
And every fair from fair sometime declines,
By chance, or nature's changing course untrimmed;
But thy eternal summer shall not fade,
Nor lose possession of that fair thou ow'st,
Nor shall death brag thou wander'st in his shade,
When in eternal lines to time thou grow'st;
So long as men can breathe, or eyes can see,
So long lives this, and this gives life to thee.

William Shakespeare

Grace was in all her steps
Heaven in her eye
In every gesture, dignity and love.

John Milton, Paradise Lost

LOVE AND NEVER FEAR

Never love unless you can
Bear with all the faults of man.
Men sometimes will jealous be
Though but little cause they see
And hang the head, as discontent
And speak what straight they will repent.

Men that but one saint adore
Make a show of love, no more.
Beauty must be scorned in none
Though but truly served in one,
For what is courtship, but disguise?
True hearts may have dissembling eyes.

Men, when their affairs require
Must awhile themselves retire;
Sometimes hunt, and sometimes hawk
And not ever sit and talk.
If these and such like you can bear
Then like, and love, and never fear.

Thomas Campion

*L*ove works for those who work at it.

ON MARRIAGE

Never marry but for love; but see that thou lovest what is lovely. He that minds a body and not a soul has not the better part of that relation and will consequently want the noblest comfort of a married life. Between a man and his wife nothing ought to rule but love. As love ought to bring them together so it is the best way to keep them well together.

A husband and wife that love and value one another show their children that they should do so too. Others visibly lose their authority in their families by their contempt of one another, and teach their children to be unnatural by their own examples.

Let not enjoyment lessen, but augment affection; it being the basest of passions to like, when we have not, what we slight when we possess. Here it is we ought to search out our pleasure of an enduring nature; sickness, poverty, or disgrace being not able to shake it, because it is not under the moving influences of worldly contingencies.

Nothing can be more entire and without reserve, nothing more zealous, affectionate and sincere, nothing more contented and constant than such a couple, nor no greater temporal felicity than to be one of them.

William Penn

Love never professes, love confesses.

Oswald Chambers

This is a delightful little song from The Sound of Music, *sung by Maria to sixteen-year-old Leisl, who had just been betrayed by her first love.*

A bell is no bell till you ring it,
A song is no song till you sing it,
And love in your heart wasn't put there to stay,
Love isn't love till you give it away.

When you're sixteen going on seventeen
Waiting for life to start
Somebody kind who touches your mind
Will suddenly touch your heart.

When that happens, after it happens
Nothing is quite the same.
Somehow you know you'll jump up and go
If ever he calls your name.

Gone are your old ideas of life
The old ideas grow dim.
Lo and behold, you're someone's wife
And you belong to him.

You may think this kind of adventure
Never may come to you.
Darling sixteen, going on seventeen,
Wait a year or two.

I'll wait a year or two.

Oscar Hammerstein II

'For love is as strong as death, and its
jealousy is as enduring as the grave. Love
flashes like fire, the brightest kind of flame.
Many waters cannot quench love; neither
can rivers drown it. If a man tried to buy
love with everything he owned, his offer
would be utterly despised.'

Song of Songs 8:6–7 (NLT)

COMMITMENT

Song of Songs 8:6–7

This ancient poem paints a lovely picture of both married love and the love God desires from his people. In a world where marriage vows are routinely broken and hearts are scarred by infidelity, commitment serves as a seal on our hearts that is never to be broken. It will not allow destructive forces into a marriage, nor will it allow tempting thoughts within us to burst out and manifest themselves in unfaithful actions. A love 'as strong as death' is a love commitment "til death us do part.' A committed love does not give way when storms of life cause the floodwaters to rise. This kind of commitment is built carefully through effort, sacrifice, and courage. It is more valuable than any material possession. Have you ever been tempted to give up on a commitment when things got tough? Resolve now, with the Lord's example as your strength (Matt. 4:1–11), to place a seal of commitment on your most important relationships.

Touchpoint – New Living Translation Bible

Give honour to marriage and remain faithful
to one another in marriage.

Hebrews 13:4 (NLT)

Successful marriage is more than finding the
right person. It is about being the right person.

Source unknown

THE PROMISE OF MARRIAGE

By my own free choice I am now committed
to your happiness, security and well being. I
will do all in my power to draw out the full
potential in you and to make our marriage
work. I will love you with a tender love. If
you have tried and failed and just need a hand
in yours in the darkness of disappointment,
you can count on mine. I am dedicated to
your growth and fulfilment as a person.

I am committed to love you with an
unconditional love. You do not have to be
fearful that love will be taken away. You will
not be punished for your openness and
honesty. There is no admission price to my
love, no rental fees or instalment payments to
be made. There may be days when

disagreements and disturbing emotions may come between us. There may be times when psychological or physical miles may lie between us. But I have given you the word of my commitment. I have set my life on a course. I will not go back on my word to you ... I will not reject you! I am committed to your growth and happiness. I'll always love you.

John Powell, Unconditional Love

Marriage is a journey, not an arrival. I love the lyrics of this song from The King and I. *It reflects so much what I felt when I was married ... that I should always support, affirm and encourage my husband, especially in times of failure and shattered dreams.*

SOMETHING WONDERFUL

This is a man who thinks with his heart –
His heart is not always wise.
This is a man who stumbles and falls,
But this is a man who tries.
This is a man you'll forgive and forgive,
And help and protect as long as you live.

He will not always say
What you would have him say
But now and then he'll say
Something wonderful.
The thoughtless things he'll do
Will hurt and worry you
Then all at once he'll do
Something wonderful.

He has a thousand dreams
That won't come true.
You know that he believes in them
And that's enough for you!

You'll always go along,
Defend him when he's wrong,
And tell him when he's strong
He is wonderful.

He'll always need your love
And so he'll get your love
A man who needs your love
Can be wonderful.

Oscar Hammerstein II

The Bible teaches us that love is not a feeling but a commitment. The gifts that come from love are many – forgiveness, patience, kindness, love for truth, justice, love for the best for a person, loyalty at any cost, belief in a person no matter what. This commitment produces the good feeling, not the other way round.

The wife described in Proverbs 31 is affectionately known as 'Mrs Proverbs' and many would aspire to her godly character. She gives the lie to the idea of Christian women being 'doormats'.

A WIFE OF NOBLE CHARACTER

Who can find a virtuous and capable wife? She is worth more than precious rubies. Her husband can trust in her, and she will greatly enrich his life. She will not hinder him but help him all her life.

She finds wool and flax and busily spins it. She is like a merchant's ship; she brings her food from afar. She gets up before dawn to prepare breakfast for her household and plan the day's work for the servant girls. She goes out to inspect a field and buys it; with her earnings she plants a vineyard.

She is energetic and strong, a hard worker. She watches for bargains; her lights burn late into the night. Her hands are busy spinning thread, her fingers twisting fibre.

She extends a helping hand to the poor

and opens her arms to the needy.

She has no fear of winter for her household because all of them have warm clothes. She quilts her own bedspreads. She dresses like royalty in gowns of finest cloth.

Her husband is well known, for he sits in the council meeting with the other civic leaders.

She makes belted linen garments and sashes to sell to the merchants.

She is clothed with strength and dignity, and she laughs with no fear of the future. When she speaks, her words are wise, and kindness is the rule when she gives instructions. She carefully watches all that goes on in her household and does not have to bear the consequences of laziness.

Her children stand and bless her. Her husband praises her: 'There are many virtuous women in the world, but you surpass them all!'

Charm is deceptive, and beauty does not last; but a woman who fears the Lord will be greatly praised. Reward her for all she has done. Let her deeds publicly declare her praise.

Proverbs 31:10–31 (NLT)

MARRIAGE

Proverbs 31:10–31

Although many ancient cultures were disrespectful of women, the woman portrayed here has become highly regarded. She is not only a wife and mother but also a businesswoman who imports goods, manages staff, and trades in real estate. Notice too that someone has made the effort to affirm her talents and character by praising her in this text. How blessed is a husband whose wife has so many abilities and such noble character. And how blessed is the wife whose husband affirms her and who is supportive of her personal development. Although sexual intimacy is important in marriage, the relationship relies heavily upon day-to-day affirmation. If you are married, think of how you can praise and support your partner today.

Touchpoint – New Living Translation Bible

A key to successful marriage is appreciation. It is
easy after a while to take each other for granted,
or to be noticed only when something hasn't been
done!

Thank you
Thank you for the care you take
In making out of our house – a home
In creating out of our living room
More than just a good room –
But a place in which my mind can be free
Can rest and be at ease ...

Thank you for the flowers on my desk
For the mended sweater
For the choice of music
With which you woke me
Thank you for granting me silence
Thank you for swallowing your words
When you noticed my inability to deal
   with yet more.

Thank you
For just taking over
When I couldn't do any more
When too much was just too much

Thank you
For your patience
Allowing me to develop at my own speed

Thank you
For sharing your fear and your joy
Your struggle, your love
And your life with me.

Ulrich Schaeffer

If we make a lifelong commitment to marriage, when troubles come we will look for a way through, not a way out.

Source unknown

We imagine the kind of person who would make us completely happy. If only he or she were thinner or fatter or wittier or stronger with the children. But when we are consumed by the idea of the kind of person we want them to be, we so often miss the person that they are. Sometimes after a marriage is over the partners will look back and wonder, 'Why were those things such a big deal to me, when he was kind and always there for me?' 'Why was her dress size more important to me than the person that she was?'

Rob Parsons, The Sixty Second Marriage

IF EVER I WOULD LEAVE YOU

If ever I would leave you, it wouldn't be in
    summer.
Seeing you in summer, I never would go.
Your hair streaked with sunlight
Your lips red as flame
Your face with a lustre that puts gold to shame.
But if I'd ever leave you it couldn't be in
    autumn.
How I'd leave in autumn I never will know
I've seen how you sparkle
When fall nips the air,
I know you in autumn
And I must be there.
And could I leave you running merrily through
    the snow,
Or on a wintry evening when you catch the
    fire's glow?
If ever I would leave you how could it be in
    springtime,
Knowing how in spring I'm bewitched by you
    so?
Oh no, not in springtime, summer, winter or
    fall,
No, never could I leave you at all.

Alan Jay Lerner, Camelot

CHAPTER FIVE

Love Lost

❀ ❀ ❀

*A*nyone who enjoyed the voice of Frank Sinatra will remember his most famous album, Songs for Swinging Lovers. It was the first album I ever owned, and I had it before I had a record player! Here is a lovely memory of those heady days.

Everybody's hand in hand, swinging down the
     lane,
Everybody's feeling grand, swinging down the
     lane.
That's the time I miss the bliss that we might
     have known,
Nights like this when I'm all alone.
When the moon is on the rise, baby, I'm so
     blue,
Watching lovers making eyes like we used to
     do.
When the moon is on the wane, still I'm
     waiting all in vain,
Should be swinging down the lane ... with you.

Isham Jones/Gus Khan

83

Of all affliction taught a lover yet
'Tis sure the hardest science to forget.

Alexander Pope

*H*ere are the lyrics of two beautiful plaintive songs
my husband recorded many years ago.

HERE'S THAT RAINY DAY

Here's that rainy day,
Maybe I should have saved those left over dreams.
Funny, but here's that rainy day,
Here's that rainy day they told me about.
And I laughed at the thought that it might turn
      out this way.

Where is that worn out wish that I threw aside
After it brought my lover near?
Funny how love becomes a cold, rainy day,
Funny, that rainy day is here.

Jimmy Van Heusen/Johnny Burke

SO WOULD I

Why am I enraptured?
Though conquered and captured,
I just hope you know what you have done.
Why am I enchanted?
Though taken for granted
And I find I'm not the only one.
… Tell me …

Why do the stars adore you?
All day they're lonesome for you
They'd give you the sky –
By the way, so would I.

Think how the raindrops miss you.
They hurry down to kiss you
And hope for a sigh.
By the way, so would I.

I saw a rose try
To imitate your smile,
And you could have heard
My heart for a country mile.

The wise old owl is scheming,
He overheard you dreaming.
And what he won't try, win or lose, do or die –
And by the way, so would I.

Jimmy Van Heusen/Johnny Burke

She dwelt among the untrodden ways
Beside the springs of Dove
A maid whom there were none to praise
And very few to love:

A violet by a mossy stone
Half-hidden from the eye!
Fair as a star, when only one
Is shining in the sky.

She lived unknown, and few could know
When Lucy ceased to be;
But she is in her grave, and, oh,
The difference to me!

William Wordsworth

*O*ne of the saddest parts of the loss of a loved one is
the 'gone forever' of the 'circling arms'. How good
that the arms of God are everlastingly there for us.

The eternal God is your refuge, and
underneath are the everlasting arms.

Deuteronomy 33:27 (NIV)

Within Thy circling arms we lie,
O God! In Thy infinity,
Our souls in quiet shall abide
Beset with love on every side.

Anon.

'The Everlasting Arms.' I think of that
whenever rest is sweet. How the whole earth
and the strength of it, that is almightiness, is
beneath every tired creature to give it rest;
holding us, as always! No thought of God is
closer than that. No human tenderness of
patience is greater than that which gathers in
its arms a little child, and holds it, heedless
of weariness. And He fills the great earth,
and all upon it, with this unseen force of His
love, that never forgets or exhausts itself, so
that everywhere we may lie down in His
bosom, and be comforted.

D. T. Whitney

'Fear not, you will no longer live in shame.
The shame of your youth and the sorrows of
widowhood will be remembered no more,
for your Creator will be your husband. The
Lord Almighty is his Name! He is your
Redeemer, the Holy One of Israel, the God
of all the earth. For the Lord has called you
back from your grief – as though you were a
young wife abandoned by her husband,' says
your God.

Isaiah 54:4–6 (NLT)

The following poem was written for a book, Love is
Still Among Us, *dedicated to the people of
Omagh in aid of 'Kids for Peace'. It is a beautiful
expression of love for those who died or were injured
in the bombing. The power of love and compassion is
very evident in the poems, many of which are written
by children.*

O FATHER, ON YOUR LOVE

O Father, on your love we call
When sorrow overshadows all
And pain that feels too great to bear
Drives from us any words for prayer.
Enfold in love for evermore
All those we love, but see no more.

Our children, innocent and dear,
Were strangers to a world of fear.
Each precious life had more to give.
In each, our hopes and dreams could live.
Enfold in love for evermore
All those we love, but see no more.

So brief the joy since each was born,
So long the years in which to mourn.
Give us compassion to sustain
Each other in this time of pain.
Enfold in love for evermore
All those we love, but see no more.

Guard us from bitterness and hate
And share with us grief's crushing weight.
Help us to live from day to day
Until, once more, we find our way.
Enfold in love for evermore
All those we love, but see no more.

When dark despair is all around
And falling tears the only sound,
Light one small flame to hope that still
You walk with us, and always will.
Enfold in love for evermore
All those we love, but see no more.

Jane Holloway, Dunblane, 13 March 1996,
Love is Still Among Us

This eulogy was written and read by William Booth at the funeral of his wife, Catherine. Have you ever wondered what someone may say about you at the end of your life?

WHEN THE END COMES

If you had a tree ... under your window, which, for forty years had been your shadow from the burning sun, whose flowers had been the adornment and beauty of your life, whose fruit had been almost the stay of your very existence ...

If you had a servant who, for all this long time, had served you without fee or reward, who had ministered, for very love, to your health and comfort ...

If you had a counsellor who in hours – continually occurring – of perplexity and amazement, had ever advised you ...

If you had had a friend who had understood your very nature, the rise and fall of your feelings, the bent of your thoughts, and the purpose of your existence; a friend whose communion had ever been pleasant – the most pleasant of all other friends, to whom you had ever turned with satisfaction ...

If you had had a mother of our children who had cradled and nursed and trained them for the service of the living God, in which you most delighted; a mother indeed ...

If you had had a wife, a sweet love of a

wife, who for forty years had never given you real cause of grief; a wife who had stood with you side by side in the battle's front, who had been a comrade to you, ever willing to interpose herself between you and the enemy and ever the strongest when the battle was fiercest ...

My comrades, roll all these qualities into one personality and what would be lost in each I have lost, all in one ... yet my heart is full of gratitude because God lent me for so long a season such a treasure.

I have never turned from her these forty years for any journeyings on my mission of mercy but I have longed to get back, and have counted the weeks, days, and hours which should take me again to her side. And now she has gone away for the last time. What, then, is left for me to do? My work is plainly to fill up the weeks, the days, the hours, and cheer my poor heart as I go along with the thought that, when I have served my Christ and my generation according to the will of God – which I vow this afternoon I will, to the last drop of my blood – then I trust she will bid me welcome to the skies, as He bade her.

William Booth

CHAPTER SIX

Family Love

❋ ❋ ❋

In Ephesians 5:18–6:4, Paul represents the three key words which identify the roles of each member of the family, and unless we clearly understand how these roles operate then we will never achieve the degree of family unity which the New Testament unfolds. The role of the husband is that of *loving leadership*, and the one of the wife is one of *joyful submission*. Children are enjoined by God to be *obedient*, for by this attitude, their characters are developed and fitted for future service in society and in the church.

Much of the trend in today's society such as unisex and 'Women's Lib' is diametrically opposed to the teaching of the Scriptures, and we Christians must make our homes distinctive by showing the world how to live successful family lives by obedience to God's commands. Edith Schaeffer says, 'Today many women are struggling against their femininity, while men are battling against their masculinity. It is Satan who is behind all this, attempting to wipe out the antithesis, along with destroying the concept of what is true and false, which is the whole teaching of relativity.'

The underlying secret of family happiness is for each person to discover the role God has ordained for them, and to function within it in the way God has appointed. The best thing a man can do for God is *to be a man* and demonstrate a strong, loving leadership in his home. The best thing a woman can do is to *be a woman* and display the graces which God has built into the feminine personality from the beginning of time.

Selwyn Hughes, Reflections

*T*he most important thing a father can do for his children is to love their mother.

Every father concerned about the true development of his child gives that child a wide scope for the exercise of judgment and decision. But he is also swift to break in at times with words of guidance and instruction which his love and longer experience qualify him to give. Guidance is therefore guidance into the highest development of our characters so that we respond to life with deep insight, clear judgment and rich understanding.

Selwyn Hughes, Reflections

*M*others hold their children's hands for a while and their hearts forever.

Every word and deed of a parent is a fibre woven into the character of a child that ultimately determines how that child fits into the fabric of society.

David Wilkerson

THE APPLAUSE OF HEAVEN

My child's feelings are hurt, I tell her she's
    special.
My child is injured, I do whatever it takes to
    make her feel better.
My child is afraid, I won't go to sleep until she is
    secure.
I'm not a hero ... I'm a parent. When a child
    hurts, a parent does what comes naturally.
    He helps ...
Why don't I let my Father do for me what I am
    more than willing to do for my own
    children?
I'm learning ... Being a father is teaching me that
    when I am criticised, injured or afraid, there
    is a Father who is ready to comfort me.
    There is a Father who will hold me until I'm
    better, help me until I can live with the hurt,
    and who won't go to sleep when I'm afraid
    of waking up and seeing the dark.
Ever.

Father, we look at your plan and see a plan
        based on love, not on our performance.
Help us to be captivated by your love.

Max Lucado

A book of childbearing is no help to an
orphan – he needs a mother.

Anon.

My dishes went unwashed today,
I didn't make the bed.
I took his hand and followed
Where his eager footsteps led.

Oh yes, we went adventuring
My little son and I ...
Exploring all the great outdoors
Beneath the summer sky.

We waded in a crystal stream,
We wandered through a wood.
My kitchen wasn't swept today
But life was gay and good.

We found a cool, sun-dappled glade
And now my small son knows
How Mother Bunny hides her nest
Where jack-in-the-pulpit grows.

We watched a robin feed her young,
We climbed a sunlit hill …
Saw cloud-sheep scamper through the sky,
We plucked a daffodil.

That my house was neglected,
That I didn't brush the stairs
In twenty years, no one on earth
Will know, or even care.

But that I've helped my little boy
To noble manhood grow
In twenty years, the whole wide world
May look and see and know.

Anon.

THE LAND OF BEGINNING AGAIN

I wish that there were some wonderful place
Called the Land of Beginning Again
Where all our mistakes and all our heartaches
And all of our selfish grief
Could be dropped like a shabby old coat by the
    door
And never be put on again.

I wish we could come on it all unaware
Like the hunter who finds a lost trail
And I wish that the one whom our blindness
    has done
The greatest injustice of all
Could be at the gates like an old friend that
    waits
For the comrade he's gladdest to hail.

We would find all the things we intended to do
But forgot, and remembered too late;
Little praises unspoken, little promises broken
And all of the thousand and one
Little duties neglected that might have
    perfected
The day for one less fortunate.

It wouldn't be possible not to be kind
In the Land of Beginning Again
And the ones we misjudged and the ones
        whom we grudged
Their moments of victory then
Would find in the grasp of our loving handclasp
More than penitent lips could explain.

For what had been hardest we'd know had
        been best
And what had seemed loss would be gain
For there isn't a sting that will not take a wing
When we've faced it and laughed it away,
And I think that the laughter is most what
        we're after
In the Land of Beginning Again.

So I wish that there were some wonderful place
Called the Land of Beginning Again
Where all our mistakes and all our heartaches
And all of our selfish grief
Could be dropped like a shabby old coat at the
        door
And never be put on again.

Louise Fletcher

WHAT GOD'S FRESH ELASTIC CAN DO

January is a fresh new month, the 'land of beginning again'. God's fresh elastic can pull you together once more. You can make a brand new start in your life. No matter what has happened in the past, that is over. No matter how much you wish the past had been different, especially concerning your wayward child, you cannot change what has already happened. Don't mourn over what is done; rejoice that there is still a future! Yesterday is a cancelled cheque, tomorrow is a promissory note but today is cash! Use it wisely. Today you can have a new refreshing love, a return to Christian fellowship, a new friendship, a new dream. Yes, you can have a fresh new start in January. Tear off that old calendar month and enjoy that fresh new page with no blot or scars on it.

God is present and ready to help you right where you are. Reach out in a simple prayer and feel Him now take your hand. With His hand and power at work in your life, you, too, can have your tears turned into joy, your night into day, your pain into gain, your failures into successes, your scars into stars, and your tragedy into triumph. Put the cancelled cheques behind you and the future in God's hands. Enjoy the cash at hand, and your new start today!

Life would be unbearable for many of us parents if it were not for the opportunity of a fresh, new beginning. Just imagine, God even designed nature to give us 365 new starts, and twelve months of fresh starts thrown in as a bonus! God made every day to be a new day!

Barbara Johnson, Fresh Elastic for
Stretched Out Moms

The best preparation for tomorrow is to do today's work superbly well.

One of the things you learn when you become a parent is the horrible thought and the reality that your children will be your children for life! That's why there's death!

Bill Cosby

When I was a boy of fourteen, my father was so ignorant I could hardly stand to have the old man around. But when I got to be twenty-one, I was astonished at how much he had learned in seven years.

Mark Twain

Ask a teenager now ... while they still know everything.

Anon.

Some years ago Nanette Newman published a delightful little book of children's quotes called Lots of Love. *In her introduction she wrote: 'Loving is the first thing children learn. I wish life would teach them never to forget it.' Here's a quote:*

You couldn't make everyone in the world love each other. They don't even get on in blocks of flats.

Lois, aged 7

'Do for others what you would like them to do for you. This is a summary of all that is taught in the law and the prophets.'

Matthew 7:12 (NLT)

TODDLERS' PROPERTY LAW

If I like it it's mine.
If it's in my hand it's mine.
If I can take it from you it's mine.
If it's mine it must never appear in any way
    to be yours.
If I'm doing or building something, all the
    pieces are mine.
If it looks like mine it's mine.
If I saw it first it's mine.
If you are playing with it and you put it
    down
It automatically becomes mine.
If it's broken it's yours.

Source unknown

The subjecting of the will (of a child) is a thing which must be done at once, and the sooner the better; for by neglecting timely correction they will contract a stubbornness and obstinacy which are hardly ever after conquered, and never without using such severity as would be painful to me as to the child. In the esteem of the world they pass for kind and indulgent, whom I call cruel parents; who permit their children to get habits which they know must afterwards be broken.

Susanna Wesley, mother of John and Charles

My mother was the source from which I derived the guiding principles of my life.

John Wesley

*S*teve Chalke's excellent book, How to Succeed as a Parent, *came too late to help me raise my children! It holds many pearls of wisdom for successful parenting.*

REMEMBER (1)

- To be happy, your children need to know that you love them unconditionally.

- Words aren't enough: what you do says much more.

- Your kids need constant reassurance that you love them for who they are, not what they do.

- Never link your love for your children with your expectations of them.

- Showing your kids that you love them no matter what lets them know they're valuable and builds up their self-esteem.

- Proving to your kids that you love them helps them cope with inevitable failure and disappointment, and gives them the confidence to try again.

REMEMBER (2)

- Becoming a parent totally transforms your life – you'll never be ready for it.

- The way a child is treated in their first few years can affect their whole life.

- Only people who aren't parents know for sure how to raise children properly.

- As a parent, you're on stage with no script and no prior rehearsals.

- However prepared you are there's no getting away from daily improvisation.

- There's no such thing as a perfect parent, but you can be a great parent.

- The most important things you need to do are work hard and trust yourself.

Steve Chalke

*N*ext are wise words from an amazing woman who, though never a mother herself, mothered thousands of people with the love of Jesus – Mother Teresa.

Today there is so much trouble in the world. I think that much of it begins at home. The world is suffering so much because there is no peace. There is no peace because there is no peace in the family and we have so many thousands and thousands of broken homes. We must make our homes centres of compassion and forgive endlessly and so bring peace.

Make your house, your family, another Nazareth where love, peace, joy and unity reign, for love begins at home. You must start here and make your home the centre of burning love, you must be the hope of eternal happiness to your wife, your husband, your child, to your grandfather, grandmother, to whoever is connected to you.

Do you know the poor of your own home first? Maybe in your home there is somebody who is feeling very lonely, very unwanted, very handicapped. Maybe your wife, your husband, your child is lonely. Do you know that?

The home is where the mother is. Once I picked up a child and took him to our children's home, gave him a bath, clean clothes, everything, but after a day the child ran away. Then I said to the Sisters, 'Please follow that child. One of you stay with him and see where he goes when he runs away.' And the child ran away a third time. There under a tree was the mother. She had put two stones under an earthenware vessel; and was cooking something she had picked up from the dustbins. The Sister asked the child, 'Why did you run away from the home?' And the child said: 'But this is my home, because this is where my mother is.'

Mother was there. That was home. That the food was taken from the dustbins was all right because mother had cooked it. It was mother that hugged the child, the mother who wanted the child, and the child had its mother. Between a wife and a husband it is the same ... Smile at one another. It is not always easy. We must give Jesus a home in our homes for only then can we give him to others.

Mother Teresa

When Mother Teresa received her Nobel Prize, she was asked, 'What can we do to promote world peace?' She replied, 'Go home and love your family.'

*J*esus told this moving story to illustrate the importance of unconditional love. When the prodigal son' recognised the mess he had made of his life he set out for home to admit it to his father. But his father saw him before he'd even reached the house and ran to greet him. He accepted him without approving of his behaviour. That is just what Jesus has done for us and we must do the same for our children.

THE LOST SONS

Jesus told them this story: 'A man had two sons. The younger son told his father, "I want my share of your estate now, instead of waiting until you die." So his father agreed to divide his wealth between his sons.

'A few days later this younger son packed all his belongings and took a trip to a distant land, and there he wasted all his money on wild living. About the time his money ran out, a great famine swept over the land, and he began to starve. He persuaded a local farmer to hire him to feed his pigs. The boy became so hungry that even the pods he was feeding the pigs looked good to him. But no one gave him anything.

'When he finally came to his senses, he said to himself, "At home even the hired men have food enough to spare, and here I am, dying of hunger! I will go home to my father and say, 'Father, I have sinned against both heaven and you, and I am no longer worthy of being called your son. Please take me on as a hired man.'"

'So he returned home to his father. And while he was still a long distance away, his father saw him coming. Filled with love and compassion, he ran to his son, embraced him, and kissed him. His son said to him, "Father, I have sinned against both heaven and you, and I am no longer worthy of being called your son."

'But his father said to the servants, "Quick! Bring the finest robe in the house and put it on him. Get a ring for his finger, and sandals for his feet. And kill the calf we have been fattening in the pen. We must celebrate with a feast, for this son of mine was dead and has now returned to life. He was lost, but now he is found." So the party began.

'Meanwhile the older son was in the fields working. When he returned home, he heard music and dancing in the house, and he asked the servants what was going on. "Your brother is back," he was told, "and your father has killed the calf we were fattening and has prepared a great feast. We are celebrating because of his safe return."

'The older brother was angry and wouldn't go in. His father came out and begged him, but he replied, "All these years I've worked hard for you and never once refused to do a single thing you told me to. And in all that time you never gave me even one young goat for a feast with my friends. Yet when this son of yours comes back after squandering your money on prostitutes, you celebrate by killing the finest calf we have."

'His father said to him, "Look, dear son, you and I are very close, and everything I have is yours. We had to celebrate this happy day, for your brother was dead and has come back to life! He was lost, but now is found!"'

Luke 15:11–32 (NLT)

The mark of a loving parent is the willingness to forgive.

John Powell

There are two 'messages' that all human beings need to receive and record. They are the messages of affirmation and personal responsibility. The two messages are like the two legs on which a person can walk successfully through life. The message of affirmation is this: 'You are a unique human being, the one and only you. You are a creature of God made in His image and likeness. But after He made you He broke the mould. There never was and never will be another you. You are a real gift to this world and a person of inestimable worth.' The message of responsibility is this: 'As you mature into adulthood you must take your life into your own hands. You must at this time assume full responsibility for your life, your emotions and attitudes. The outcome of your life is in your hands. When you look into a mirror, you are looking at the one person who is responsible for your happiness.'

Someone has compared these messages to 'roots and wings'. We must give to others both roots and wings. The roots of any human existence are the roots of personal worth, of self-confidence, the roots of belief in one's own uniqueness. The message that offers roots is that of unconditional love. The wings of a human existence are the wings of self-responsibility. Giving a person wings is the message that, 'You have everything you need to soar, to sing your own song, to warm the world with your presence. The direction of your flight, that song you will sing and the warmth you will bestow on this world are your responsibility. You must take your life into your own hands. You must not blame others and complain about your lack of opportunity. You must assume full responsibility for the course and direction of your life.' The message of roots says to an individual: 'You've got it!' The message of wings says: 'Now go for it!'

John Powell

I turned to bribery via magnificent and thoroughly unsuitable gifts: a shining bicycle when he was too young to use it ... when he wanted to play basketball, a set of gloves and masks and bats and uniforms that the Yankees would have envied. I confess it. I gave him everything but myself.

Edward G. Robinson

Too much love never spoils children. Children become spoiled when we substitute 'presents' for 'presence'.

Dr Anthony P. Witham

An infallible way to make your child miserable is to satisfy all his demands.

Henry Home

To discipline and reprimand a child produces wisdom, but a mother is disgraced by an undisciplined child.

Proverbs 29:15 (NLT)

*R*ob Parsons, Director of Care for the Family, was inspired to write the following poem after a conversation he'd had with Roy about cleaning our children's shoes. Roy was so pleased with it he read it at a concert at the London Palladium.

A MAN LOOKS BACK

I always cleaned the children's shoes,
The little (tiny) patent shoes
That covered feet fresh out of booties.
Cleaned the black and made it shine
Removing final traces of stewed prune
And other culinary delights – known only
  to the very young.

And as they grew I cleaned a larger shoe,
Shoes that were strong enough to walk in
  (almost!)
Certainly strong enough for a toddler to
  take five steps … and …
And then the first school shoes,
Shoes that led such little feet
Into a world full of such tomorrows.

And later shoes, the toes of which
Lost all their battles with footballs,
  gravel, and old tin cans –
New shoes, that looked old within a
  week …

I cleaned them all.

And as each night I did the task
A million memories came flooding back
And I remembered a man long since gone
Would clean our shoes.
Six children in all – my father cleaned
     each one –
As I now shine these for mine.

But children grow
And shoes are for feet that move –
That take the boy into a man.
And I remember well, the evening that I
     came
With cloth and brush
As I had done so many times –
Only to discover that of course the shoes
     had gone.

But they will come again, those shoes,
Come again to me – oh, not for cleaning
     now,
Other hands have long since done that
     task –
No, they will bring a man to me and a
     woman
Holding the hands of tiny ones
With little feet.

And young eyes will look up and say,
'Grandpa, Mummy said … that you will
     clean my shoes.'

Rob Parsons

When our children were young, (it was before the days of camcorders) my husband would leave the tape recorder running during a meal or while they were playing. The results were priceless and even today bring so much laughter and precious memories to our family. I was delighted, therefore, to discover the following conversation, from one of Spike Milligan's books.

CHRISTMAS 1959

On Christmas Eve 1959 I placed a recording machine in my children's bedroom after I turned the lights out. Alas, at one stage the machine broke down but this is a verbatim record of my three children's conversation, Laura aged seven, Sean aged five and Sile aged three and a half.

Laura: We must hurry up and go to sleep.
SILENCE
Sile: Did you heered dat, dat was I being quiet for Farder Christmas.
Laura: Shhhhhhh. I can hear someone coming!
Sean: It's not me, I'm already here.
Laura: Shhhhhhhh, Sean!
Sean: I am shushinggg, listen …
SILENCE
Sile: Do bunny rabbits have Quickmass?
Laura: Oh, hurry up and stop talking.
Sean: It wasunt me, I stopped talking ten hours ago.

Sile: Dat wasunt me talking, dat was Sean.

Laura: Father Christmas won't come if we
are not asleeped.

Sile: Doesn't he like awake children?

Laura: Yes but only if they are asleeped.

Sean: I'm asleep now but I can still talk.

Laura: (CALLING) Dadddyyy …
Daddyyyyyyyy.

ENTER FATHER

Me: What is it?

Laura: They won't go asleep.

Me: Listen, children, if you don't go to sleep
Father Christmas won't stop here.

Sean: Where will he stop?

Me: Oh, er, somewhere else.

Sean: I wish we lived there.

Me: Now be good and go to sleep …
Goodnight.

OMNES: Goodnight, Daddy.

SILENCE

Sile: Shhhhhhhhhh – I think he's coming.

Sean: Tell him not yet, I'm still awake.

Sile: So am I, you can hear me being awake.

Laura: (DESPERATE) Ohhh, go to
sleeppppppppp. Go to
sleeppppppppppppppppp.

Sile: I'm going to sleep.

SILENCE

Sean: I can't hear you.

Sile: I'm sleeping with no noise.

Laura: Sean! Sile! Go to sleep.

Sile: I can't go to sleep as quick as you 'cause
I'm smaller.

End of Tape
Merry Christmas, Folks!

Spike Milligan, Scunthorpe Revisited, Added Articles
and Instant Relatives

Out of Heaven and just like me?
Did'st Thou sometimes think of there
And ask where all the angels were?
I should think that I would cry
For my house all made of sky
I would look about the air
And wonder where the angels were
And at waking 'twould distress me
Not an angel there to dress me.
Hadst Thou ever any toys?
Like us little girls and boys?
And didst Thou play in Heaven with all
The Angels that were not too tall
With stars for marbles? Did the things
Play 'Can you see me?' through their wings?
And did Thy mother let Thee spoil
Thy robes with playing on our soil?
How nice to have them always new
In Heaven, because 'twas quite clean blue!

Francis Thompson

These moving words were read by a friend of mine, at the thanksgiving service for her stillborn daughter, Hannah Louise.

Hannah Louise Cranefield, born 13 May 1996

Thank you, Father God, for Hannah. She was and always will be our little girl, our firstborn. She came into our lives at the right time. She brought us joy and helped us love and hope. We felt her move and kick about, she made us laugh and wonder. We thought she was a boy. We called her 'Widget' and grew to know and love her more each day. Sometimes we worried about her and our future together – about whether we could afford her, what pushchair would be best, whether we'd be good parents and whether she'd be 'normal' whatever 'normal' is – parents are allowed to worry! We prayed for her too – that she would know you. Some prayed that she would be a leader; we prayed that she would be holy and lead others to you with gentleness.

We didn't expect her to die. It seemed cruel and like everyone else we wondered why. It didn't seem fair or right. Yet, Father, if she did die and was born in the wrong order, somehow we know you let it happen for a reason and that the time was right. She was so beautiful, thin lips, her long, long lashes and gingery hair. Her little fingers and toes – a mixture of both of us without the bad bits! She weighed 7lbs 6oz. We still have her footprint and handprint and some photos but they're not the Hannah we saw. While some still think her life was wasted, we thank you for her and anticipate the ways others will be touched by her short life. It was hard to say 'Goodbye' and let her go. Death sounds so final. But no ... Hannah's life goes on. Her body has died and so in time will ours. Yet in this short time since she was born she has touched more people and brought us more meaning, hope and perspective than many ever will. Through her death we have known your love, your presence, your comfort, your peace. She brought out the love and tenderness in so many people and we pray that those who share our grief will also share our joy and peace. Deep sorrow. Deep joy. Help us not to love her any less or any more than other children you might give us. Thank you for those who comforted and loved us, but most of all – thank you for the gift of Hannah.

Sharon Cranefield, 14 May 1996

MONDAY MORNING

In my anxious sleep
You wake up smiling
Just another day for me
A new day for you.

As I grunt in the morning
You're already smiling
I lift my eyebrows at the TV news
You throw your breakfast across the room.

As I set the answerphone
And run for the bus
You commence a very different journey
The world's red carpet is laid at your feet.

And, crawling, stumbling
In a weaving line
Amid cries of delight
You take your first steps …
(I sip the third coffee of the day)
You'll sleep …
Eat …
Eat and sleep …
As I run; strive to get everything done.
And when I throw off my jacket at the end
      of the day
The joys of tomorrow are your jumbled
      dreams

Don't change, Adam
But teach me to be like you
Wordless and peaceful in a world ever new.

Ian Cranefield, written to his nephew Adam,
brother of Hannah Louise

CHAPTER SEVEN

Love for Animals

❋ ❋ ❋

*I*t has been said that Britain is a nation of animal lovers, and that no home is complete without an animal! We had several furry friends over the years including dogs and gerbils, not to mention goldfish … Many parents would agree that although you give animals to children as gifts, they look after them for a week and you look after them for the rest of their lives!

He prayeth well, who loveth well
Both man and bird and beast.
He prayeth best who loveth best
All things both great and small,
For the dear God who loveth us
He made and loveth all.

Samuel Taylor Coleridge,
'The Rime of the Ancient Mariner'

Desert creatures will meet with hyenas,
and wild goats will bleat to each other;
there the night creatures will also find
    repose
and find for themselves places of rest.
The owl will nest there and lay eggs,
she will hatch them and care for her young
    under the shadow of her wings;
there also the falcons will gather,
each with its mate.
Look in the scroll of the Lord and read:

None of these will be missing,
not one will lack her mate.
For it is his mouth that has given the order,
and his Spirit will gather them together.
He allots their portions;
his hand distributes them by measure.
They will possess it forever
and dwell there from generation to
    generation.

Isaiah 34:14–17 (NIV)

On that day HOLY TO THE LORD will be
inscribed on the bells of the horses.

Zechariah 14:20 (NIV)

All animals are equal, but some animals are
more equal than others.

George Orwell

*I am including the following poem in gratitude to my
long-suffering editor Judith Longman who adores
cats.*

Long may you love your pensioner mouse
Though one of a tribe that torment the house
Nor dislike for her cruel sport the cat
Deadly foe both of mouse and rat:
Remember she follows the law of her kind
And instinct is neither wayward nor blind
Then think of her beautiful gliding form
Her tread that would scarce crush a worm
And her soothing song by the winter fire
Soft as the dying throb of the lyre.

William Wordsworth

It's hard to believe, but some people claim
their cats are almost human – and they mean
it as a compliment!

Anon.

I learnt this beautiful poem as a child and have
never forgotten it. Many people will know it now
as the piece by John Tavener which was sung at the
funeral of Diana, Princess of Wales.

THE LAMB

Little lamb who made thee?
Dost thou know who made thee?
Gave thee life and bid thee feed
By the stream and o'er the mead;
Gave thee clothing of delight,
Softest clothing, woolly bright;
Gave thee such a tender voice
Making all the vales rejoice?
Little lamb who made thee?
Dost thou know who made thee?

Little lamb, I'll tell thee
Little lamb, I'll tell thee
He is callèd by thy name
For He calls Himself a lamb.
He is meek and He is mild,
He became a little child.
I a child and thee a lamb
We are called by His Name.
Little lamb, God bless thee;
Little lamb, God bless thee.

William Blake

*M*aking up limericks was one of the many ways to
entertain our children during long car journeys.
Here's an animal one by the brilliant Michael Palin.

There was a tortoise called Joe
Whose progress was painfully slow.
He'd stop for a week,
Look around, take a peek,
Then unlike a shot, off he'd go.

Michael Palin

THE WAY THROUGH THE WOODS

They shut the road through the woods
Seventy years ago.
Weather and rain have undone it again,
And now you would never know
There was once a road through the woods
Before they planted the trees.
It is underneath the coppice and heath
And the thin anemones.
Only the keeper sees
That, where the ring-dove broods,
And the badgers roll at ease,
There was once a road through the woods.

Yet, if you enter the woods
Of a summer evening late,
When the night-air cools on the trout-
    ringed pools
Where the otter whistles his mate.
(They fear not men in the woods
Because they see so few)
You will hear the beat of a horse's feet
And the swish of a skirt in the dew,
Steadily cantering through
The misty solitudes,
As though they perfectly knew
The old lost road through the woods …
But there is no road through the woods.

Rudyard Kipling

*Here's a classic by the master of limericks –
Edward Lear.*

THE OWL AND THE PUSSY CAT

The Owl and the Pussy-Cat went to sea
In a beautiful pea-green boat,
They took some honey, and plenty of money,
Wrapped up in a five-pound note.
The Owl looked up to the stars above
And sang to a small guitar,
'O lovely Pussy! O Pussy, my love,
What a beautiful Pussy you are.
You are,
You are!
What a beautiful Pussy you are!'

Pussy said to the Owl, 'You elegant fowl!
How charmingly sweet you sing!
O let us be married! Too long we have tarried
But what shall we do for a ring?'
They sailed away for a year and a day
To the land where the Bong-tree grows
And there in the wood a piggy-wig stood
With a ring at the end of his nose,
His nose,
His nose.
With a ring at the end of his nose.

'Dear Pig, are you willing to sell for one shilling
Your ring?' Said the piggy, 'I will.'
So they took it away, and were married next day
By the Turkey who lives on the hill.
They dined on mince, and plenty of quince
Which they ate with a runcible spoon;
And hand in hand, on the edge of the sand
They danced by the light of the moon,
The moon,
The moon.
They danced by the light of the moon.

Edward Lear

PIED BEAUTY

Glory be to God for dappled things –
For skies of couple-colour as a brinded cow;
For rose-moles all in stipple upon trout that swim;
Fresh-firecoal chestnut-falls; finches' wings;
Landscape plotted and pieced – fold, fallow, and
        plough;
And all trades, their gear and tackle and trim.
All things counter, original, spare, strange;
Whatever is fickle, freckled (who knows how?)
With swift, slow; sweet, sour; adazzle, dim;
He fathers-forth whose beauty is past change:
Praise him.

Gerard Manley Hopkins

In that day the wolf and the lamb will live together; the leopard and the goat will be at peace. Calves and yearlings will be safe among lions, and a little child will lead them all. The cattle will graze among bears. Cubs and calves will lie down together. And lions will eat grass as the livestock do. Babies will crawl safely among poisonous snakes. Yes, a little child will put its hand in a nest of deadly snakes and pull it out unharmed. Nothing will hurt or destroy in all my holy mountain. And as the waters fill the sea, so the earth will be filled with people who know the LORD.

Isaiah 11:6–9 (NLT)

CHAPTER EIGHT

Friendship Love

✳ ✳ ✳

A friend is a gift you give yourself.

Robert Louis Stevenson

How many friends do you have? We might have many acquaintances; we might have 'fair-weather' friends who are happy to know us in our success, but who run at the first sign of trouble! Real friends are few and very precious. Friends share affection, companionship, joys and sorrows, confidences, kindnesses, support, trust and understanding.

I have a few friends I have known for most of my lifetime and though we may not be able to see each other often, we pick up as if it were yesterday. A precious treasure indeed!

A man of many companions may come to ruin, but there is a friend who sticks closer than a brother.

Proverbs 18:24 (NIV)

The story of friendship
Is not the outstretched hand
Not the kindly smile
Nor the joy of companionship;
It's the spiritual inspiration
That comes to one
When he discovers
That someone believes in him
And is willing to trust him
With his friendship.

Ralph Waldo Emerson

A friend is always loyal, and a brother is born
to help in time of need.

Proverbs 17:17 (NLT)

I heard of a young woman who sought a counsellor's advice because she was lonely and needed a friend. The counsellor asked her what qualities she would want to find in that friend. The young woman named some of these qualities, to which the counsellor replied, 'Go and be that person for someone else.'

> Dear friends, since God has loved us that much, we surely ought to love each other. No one has ever seen God. But if we love each other, God lives in us, and his love has been brought to full expression through us.

> *1 John 4:11 (NLT)*

There have been times in my life when I felt I needed a friend to help me sort out a particular problem and have cried out to God on my knees for such help. But it has always been tempered with 'If you want me to share it with someone, Lord, please cause someone to phone me.' If the phone call hasn't come, I have heard the Lord gently nudge me and say, 'But I'm here and listening – isn't that enough?'

> As much as possible, friends need to be available to one another. It takes time to beat a path from one heart to another – time spent laughing, talking, listening, and helping. But if we begin feeling that we must be there in every need, available in every

crisis, we could use a reminder that there is only one Friend capable of that.

Once I was conducting an important meeting in my home when the phone rang. It was a friend urgently in need of a listening ear. Quietly I said, 'I have a house full of people here right now, so I can't talk, but you know that I care. I love you and I'll call you back as soon as this meeting's over.'

When I returned her call she said, 'Thank you for taking time to say you care and to remind me of your love. You can't know how much it meant to hear that at that moment. And thank you for saying you'd call back – and then doing it. But a funny thing happened. When you weren't available, I went to my knees and had a very precious time with the Lord. I'm OK now.'

What a wonderful reminder that, whether through us or around us, it is always and only our Lord who meets needs. He is there when we are and when we aren't. How precious when he slips through the gate and down the path to a friend's heart, quietly embracing needs in his arms of sufficiency.

Susan Lenzkes

Show me a friend who will weep with me; those who will laugh with me I can find myself.

Yugoslav proverb

There is a delightful book written by Oscar Wilde, called The Selfish Giant. *I loved reading it to my children at bedtime, but never could read it without crying! It is a story about an unkind giant, who hated children, but he has his heart melted by a little child who appears one day in his garden. He subsequently allows all the village children to play in his garden, but the little boy never reappears, and no one knows what happened to him until one day he returns when the giant is very old and feeble ...*

In the farther corner of the garden
Was a tree quite covered with lovely white
    blossoms.
Its branches were golden
And silver fruit hung down from them,
and underneath it stood the little boy he had
    loved.
Downstairs ran the Giant in great joy
And out into the garden.
He hastened across the grass
And came near the child.
And when he came quite close the Giant's
    face grew red with anger
And he said, 'Who hath dared to wound
    thee?'
For on the palms of the child's hands were the
    prints of two nails
And the prints of two nails were on the little
    feet.
'Who hath dared to wound thee?' cried the
    Giant,

'Tell me, that I may take my sword and slay
   him!'
'Nay,' answered the child, 'but these are the
   wounds of Love.'
'Who art thou?' said the Giant, and a strange
   awe fell on him
And he knelt before the little child.
And the child smiled on the giant
And said to him,
'You let me play once in your garden,
Today you shall come with me to my garden,
Which is Paradise.'
And when the children ran in that afternoon
They found the Giant lying dead under the
   tree,
All covered with white blossoms.

Oscar Wilde

A good deed is never lost; he who sows
courtesy reaps friendship, and he who plants
kindness gathers love.

St Basil

For whatsoever a man soweth, that shall he also reap ... And let us not be weary in well doing: for in due season we shall reap, if we faint not.

Galatians 6:7, 9 (AV)

Goodness is something so simple; always to live for others, never to seek one's own advantage.

Dag Hammarskjöld

The ministry of kindness is a ministry which may be achieved by all men, rich and poor, learned and illiterate. Brilliance of mind and capacity for deep thinking have rendered great service to humanity, but by themselves they are impotent to dry a tear or mend a broken heart.

Anon.

The final results of our lives will be in what we have done for people, not in our possessions.

Anon.

This beautiful song comes from the film, Prince of Egypt. *If only we could see our lives from God's perspective, I think we would live very differently.*

THROUGH HEAVEN'S EYES

A single thread in a tapestry though its
    colours brightly shine
Can never see its purpose in the pattern of
    the grand design.
And the stone that sits on the very top of the
    mountain's mighty face
Does it think it's more important than the
    stones that form the base?

So how can you see what your life is worth?
Or where your value lies?
You can never see through the eyes of man
You must look at your life
Look at your life through Heaven's eyes.

A lake of gold in the desert sand is less than a
    cool fresh spring
And to one lost sheep a shepherd boy is
    greater than the richest king.
If a man loses everything he owns has he
    truly lost his worth?
Or is it the beginning of a new and brighter
    birth?

So how do you measure the worth of a man?
In wealth or strength or size?
In how much he gained or how much he
      gave?
The answer will come
The answer will come to him who tries
To look at his life through Heaven's eyes.

And that's why we share all we have with you
Though there's little to be found.
When all you've got is nothing
There's a lot to go around.
No life can escape being blown about
By the winds of change and chance.
And though you never know all the steps
You must learn to join the dance
You must learn to join the dance.

So how do you judge what a man is worth?
By what he builds or buys?
You can never see with your eyes on earth;
Look through Heaven's eyes
Look at your life, look at your life
Look at your life through Heaven's eyes.

Stephen Schwartz

Now we see but a poor reflection as in a mirror; then we shall see face to face. Now I know in part; then I shall know fully, even as I am fully known.

1 Corinthians 13:12 (NIV)

One of the most awesome poems I know was given to me shortly after I became a Christian. Its content had a profound effect on me, giving me boldness to speak out about what Jesus had done for me, so that others would have the opportunity to discover this love too.

MY FRIEND

My friend, I stand in the judgment and feel that
    you're to blame somehow ...
On earth, I walked with you day by day and
    never did you point the way.
You knew the Lord in truth and glory, but
    never did you tell the story.
My knowledge then was very dim; you could
    have led me safe to him.
Though we lived together on the earth, you
    never told me of the second birth.
You taught me things, that's true, I called you
    'friend' and trusted you,
But now I learn and it's too late, you could
    have kept me from this fate.

We walked by day and talked by night, and yet
    you showed me not the light.
You let me live, and love, and die; you knew I'd
    never live on high.
Yes, I called you 'friend' in life, and trusted you
    through joy and strife
And yet, on coming to the end, I cannot now
    call you 'my friend'.

Anon.

'My prayer is not for them [his disciples] alone. I pray also for those who will believe in me through their message, that all of them may be one, Father, just as you are in me and I am in you. May they also be in us so that the world may believe that you have sent me.'

Jesus' prayer from John 17:20 (NIV)

Friends share all things.

Pythagoras

Today, I commit myself to motivating people with love rather than motivating them with fear.

Our love must be expressed in unfailing friendship. Being an understanding and caring friend may well be our most Christ-like act.

Friendship has become a lightweight word in our time. Not so in the Scriptures. It was the highest affirmation of Abraham that he was called the friend of God. Jesus ushered his disciples into a sublime level of intimacy. To be Christ's friend means befriending others.

Paul lists very specific ways to express that friendship. We are to be kind in communicating real affection for the people we want to help. That means telling people how important they are to us, how much we value them and how fervently we believe in them and their potential.

We are to treat them as brothers or sisters who long for the Lord's best in their lives. Time with them is given high priority. Listening and caring about their needs honours them as persons.

We are to be available, quick to respond to their call for help without hesitation. Night or day we are to be on call as truly reliable friends of those we are seeking to help and inspire.

Is this too much to ask? Not if we think of the people we're trying to help in the context of serving the Lord.

The thought that Christ may come to us in the very people who sometimes frustrate us the most – in the people we want to change – fills us with awe. How we respond to them is really our response to Christ. But the liberating assurance is that he will give us the love for people that's required to motivate them.

Lloyd Ogilvie, Turn Your Struggles into Stepping Stones

Let us then be what we are
And speak what we think
And in all things
Keep ourselves loyal to truth
And in the sacred professions
Of friendship.

Henry Wadsworth Longfellow

BE FULL OF LOVE

I am giving a new commandment to you now – love each other just as much as I love you. Show deep love for each other, for love makes up for many of your faults. Love overlooks insults.

When you are praying, first forgive anyone you are holding a grudge against, so that your Father in heaven will forgive you your sins too. Love your enemies! Do good to them. Lend to them. And don't be concerned about the fact that they won't repay. Do not rejoice when your enemy meets trouble. Let there be no gladness when he falls. Don't repay evil for evil. Don't snap back at those who say unkind things about you. Instead, pray for God's help for them, for we are to be kind to others, and God will bless us for it. Be kind to each other, tender-hearted, forgiving one another, just as God has forgiven you because you belong to Christ.

Little children, let us stop saying we love people; let us really love them, and show it by our actions. Then we will know for sure, by our actions, that we are on God's side, our consciences will be clear, even when we stand before the Lord.

Living Light

THE WORST DISEASE

I have come more and more to realise that being unwanted is the worst disease that any human being can ever experience. Nowadays we have found medicine for leprosy, and lepers can be cured. There's medicine for TB and consumption can be cured. But for the unwanted, except there are willing hands to serve and there's a loving heart to love, I don't think this terrible disease can be cured.

Mother Teresa

Philip Yancey in his brilliant book Where Is God When It Hurts? *talks about the incredible nervous system of the human body and the response of pain. Here he quotes Dr Paul Brand who has made a life-long study of leprosy and worked among leprosy sufferers.*

Pain is the very mechanism that forces me to stop and pay attention to the hurting member. The healthiest body is the one that feels the pain of its weakest parts. In the same way, we members of Christ's body should learn to attend to the pains of the rest of the body. In so doing we become an incarnation of Christ's risen body.

Dr Paul Brand has developed this idea as a key part of his personal philosophy. Individual cells had to give up their autonomy and learn to suffer with one another before effective multicellular organisms could be produced and survive. The same designer went on to create the human race with a new and higher purpose in mind. Not only would the cells within an individual cooperate with one another, but the individuals within the race would now move on to a new level of community responsibility, to a new kind of relationship with one another and with God.

As in the body, so in this new kind of relationship the key to success lies in the sensation of pain. All of us rejoice at the harmonious working of the human body. Yet we can but sorrow at the relationships between men and women. In human society *we are suffering because we do not suffer enough*.

So much of the sorrow in the world is due to the selfishness of one living organism that simply doesn't care when the next one suffers. In the body if one cell or group of cells grows and flourishes at the expense of the rest, we call it cancer and know that if it is allowed to spread the body is doomed. And yet, the only alternative to the cancer is absolute loyalty of every cell to the body, the head. God is calling us today to learn from the lower creation and move on to a higher level of evolution and to participate in this community which He is preparing for the salvation of the world.

Philip Yancey

I sought my soul, my soul I could not see;
I sought my God, my God eluded me;
I sought my brother – and I found all three.

Anon.

The Calcutta house of the Missionaries of Charity is bursting at the seams; and as each new house is opened there are volunteers clamouring to go there.

As the whole story of Christendom shows, if everything is asked for, everything – and more – will be accorded; if little, then nothing. It is curious, when this is so obvious, that nowadays the contrary proposition should seem the more acceptable, and endeavour directed towards softening the austerities of the service of Christ and reducing its hazards with a view to attracting people into it. After all, it was in kissing a leper's hideous sores that St Francis found the gaiety to captivate the world and gather round him the most audacious spirits of the age, to whom he offered only the glory of being naked on the naked earth for Christ's sake. If the demands had been less, so would the response have been. I should never have believed it possible, knowing India as I do over a number of years, to induce Indian girls of good family to tend outcasts and untouchables brought in from Calcutta streets, yet this, precisely, is the very task that Mother Teresa gives them to do when they come to her as postulants. They do it, not just in obedience, but cheerfully and ardently, and gather round her in even greater numbers for the privilege of doing it.

Accompanying Mother Teresa as we did, to these different activities for the purpose of filming them – to the Home for the Dying, to the lepers and unwanted children, I found I went through three phases. The first was horror mixed with pity, the second compassion pure and simple, and the third, reaching far beyond compassion, something I had never experienced before – an awareness of these dying and derelict men and women, these lepers with stumps instead of hands, these unwanted children, were not pitiable, repulsive or forlorn, but rather dear and delightful; as it might be, friends of long standing, brothers and sisters. How is it to be explained – the very heart and mystery of the Christian faith? To soothe these battered old heads, to grasp those poor stumps, to take in one's arms those children consigned

to dustbins, because it is His head, they are
His stumps and His children, of whom He
said that whosoever received one such child
in His Name received Him.

Malcolm Muggeridge

Lord, why did you tell me to love all men, my
    brothers?
I have tried, but I come back to you, frightened ...
Lord, I was so peaceful at home, I was so
    comfortably settled.
It was well furnished and I felt cosy
I was alone, I was at peace
Sheltered from the wind, the rain, the mud.
I should have stayed unsullied in my ivory tower
But, Lord, you have discovered a breach in my
    defences
You have forced me to open the door;
Like a squall of rain in the face, the cry of men has
    wakened me
Like a gale of wind a friendship has shaken me
As a ray of light slips in unnoticed, your grace has
    stirred me ...
And rashly enough, I left my door ajar. Now,
    Lord, I am lost.
Outside men were lying in wait for me.
I did not know they were so near; in this house; in
    this street, in

This office; my neighbour; my colleague, my
　　friend.
As soon as I started to open the door I saw them,
　　with outstretched
Hands, burning eyes, longing hearts, like beggars
　　on church steps.

Michel Quoist

It's hard to relate, Lord.
People in need. Millions of people.
Whether they're refugees, or leprosy sufferers,
　　or people without food.
Living in countries I don't know.
Names I can't pronounce in languages I don't
　　understand.
They're a long way away, just pictures.
Cardboard cut-outs, with no more reality
Than the picture on the back of a Kellogg's
　　packet.
Even those nearer to home are distant from my
　　experience.
Statistics.
There's safety in numbers:
I can forget the humanity behind them.

Men, women and children, who feel, laugh and cry.
Not much laughter though, more crying.
Tears watering the parched ground, irrigating seeds
    of pain.
The only crop that grows in the desert.

I could hide behind the questions.
Why does it happen? Why so much suffering?
I could blame others.
Politicians. Exploiters. Arms salesmen.
Multinational corporations. Currency manipulators.
That's fashionable – and true.
Why, Lord?
I hide behind the questions, and do nothing.
Waiting for an answer, because I'm scared.
    Overwhelmed. Frightened to get involved.
Like turning away from a drunk in the gutter.
And who is my neighbour? I can't argue, Lord, I
    know.
And the Absent Samaritan?
Yes, Lord, I know that too.

I know the answer has to begin with me.
Maybe I can't do a lot (more than I know, did you
    say?)
But I can do something.
Together with others, together with you
I can spread your love around.
Show me how.
So that through me, today,
Someone may catch a glimpse of your love.
May find a new life and hope.
May find the open door into your kingdom.

And, Lord, as I pray for people in need,
As I hear the crying far away,
Let me not be deaf to the cry next door.

Eddie Askew, Disguises of Love

As long as anyone has the means of doing
good to his neighbours, and does not do so,
he shall be reckoned a stranger to the love of
the Lord.

Irenaeus

CHAPTER NINE

Love for Life

* * *

It's a very short trip – while alive – live.

Source unknown

IF I HAD MY LIFE TO LIVE OVER

– written after the author found out she was dying
from cancer

I would have gone to bed when I was sick instead
of pretending the earth would go into a
holding pattern if I weren't there for the day.
I would have burned the pink candle sculpted like
a rose before it melted in storage.
I would have talked less and listened more.
I would have invited friends over to dinner even if
the carpet was stained or the sofa faded.
I would have eaten the popcorn in the 'good'
living room and worried much less about the
dirt when someone wanted to light a fire in
the fireplace.
I would have taken the time to listen to my
grandfather ramble about his youth.
I would have shared more of the responsibility
carried by my husband.

I would have never insisted the car windows be
rolled up on a summer day because my hair
had just been teased and sprayed.

I would have sat on the lawn with my children and
not have worried about grass stains.

I would have cried and laughed less while
watching television and more while watching
life.

I would never have bought anything just because
it was practical, wouldn't show soil, or was
guaranteed to last a lifetime.

Instead of wishing away nine months of
pregnancy, I'd have cherished every moment
and realised that the wonderment growing
inside me was the only chance in life to assist
God in a miracle.

When the kids kissed me impetuously, I would
have never said, 'Later, now go get washed for
dinner.'

There would have been more 'I love yous', more
'I'm sorrys',

But mostly, given another shot at life, I would
seize every minute … look at it and really see
it … live it … and never give it back.

Stop sweating the small stuff. Don't worry about
who doesn't like you, who has more or who's
doing what.

Instead, let's cherish the relationships we have
with those who do love us.

Let us think about what GOD has blessed us with.

And what we are doing each day to promote
ourselves mentally, physically, emotionally, as
well as spiritually.

Life is too short to let it pass you by. We have only this one shot at this and then it's gone. I hope you all have a blessed day.

Erma Bombeck

Keep laughing – remember it's only for life!

Source unknown

I walked a mile with pleasure and she chatted all the way
But left me none the wiser, for all she had to say.
I walked a mile with sorrow and ne'er a word said she;
But oh, the things I learned from her when sorrow walked with me.

Anon.

*A*listair Begg, a pastor in Cleveland, Ohio, and a brilliant Bible teacher, in one of his teachings on the life of Joseph said:

> When we shun trials we miss blessings. When all we have is sunshine, all we have is desert. More spiritual progress is made through failure and tears than is made through success and laughter.

> *Alistair Begg*

> Four things come not back: the spoken word, the sped arrow, time past, the neglected opportunity.

> *Anon.*

> Today is not a dress rehearsal – it's the real thing!

> *Eleanor Fulton*

The world is too much with us; late and soon,
Getting and spending, we lay waste our powers:
Little we see in Nature that is ours;
We have given our hearts away.

William Wordsworth

*Ivor Novello wrote some of the most beautiful music
of the first half of the twentieth century. I used to
enjoy singing some of his songs and this was one of
my favourites, filled with the joy of life!*

WALTZ OF MY HEART

The lark is singing on high,
The sun's ashine in the blue,
The winter is driven away
And spring is returning anew.

Who cares what sorrow may bring,
What storms may tear us apart?
No sadness can kill
The wonder and thrill of that
    waltz in my heart.
Waltz of my heart,
Haunting and gay,
Calling enthrallingly,
Waltzing away.
Ring out your bells for me,
Ivory keys;
Weave out your spells for me,
Orchestra, please.

Chorus of wings,
Filling the sky,
While you're inspiring me,
Time hurries by.
Joy fans a flame in me
Soon as you start
Sweeping your strings,
Waltz of my heart.

Words by Ivor Novello and Christopher Hassell

THE WORD FOR TODAY

Imagine a bank that credits your account each morning with £86,400, and every evening takes back what you didn't use. What would you do? Draw out every penny and invest it, of course! Well, this morning, God credited you with 86,400 seconds! (The number in one day.) Tonight, He'll write off as 'lost' what you didn't invest. You can't accumulate any of it and you can't borrow against tomorrow; you can live only on today's deposit.

Make the most of this day, for the clock is running. Before you know it you'll make your last withdrawal on the Bank of Time and stand before God. David said:'Teach us to number our days aright, that we may gain a heart of wisdom' (Psalm 90:12).

To realise the value of a year, ask the student

who just failed an exam; or the value of a
month, ask the mother who just gave birth
to a premature baby; or the value of an hour,
ask lovers who are just waiting to be
together; or the value of a minute, ask the
person who just missed a train; or the value
of a second, ask the one who just missed an
accident; or the value of a millisecond, ask
the athlete who had to settle for second
place in the Olympics.

Stop messing around! Get serious about
your life and your goals and 'make the most
of every chance you get' (Ephesians 5:16,
The Message).

Bob Gass, from The Word for Today

Life is half spent before we know what it is.

Source unknown

If you doubt the megaphone value of
suffering, I recommend that you visit the
intensive care ward of a hospital. There you'll
find all sorts of people pacing the lobby; a
mixture of rich, poor, beautiful, plain, black,
white, smart, dull, spiritual, atheistic, white
collar, blue collar. But the intensive care ward
is the one place in the world where none of
these divisions make a speck of difference.

In an intensive care ward, all visitors are

united by a single, awful thread; concern over a dying relative or friend. Economic differences, even religious differences, fade away. You'll see no sparks of racial tension there. Sometimes strangers will console one another or cry together quietly and un-ashamedly. All are facing life at its most essential. Many call for a pastor or priest for the first time ever. Only the megaphone of suffering is strong enough to bring these people to their knees to ponder ultimate questions of life and death and meaning. As Helmut Thielicke has wryly observed, there is hospital chaplaincy, but no cocktail-party chaplaincy.

That, I believe, is the megaphone value of suffering. This planet emits a constant 'groaning', a cry for redemption and restor-ation, but very often we ignore the message until suffering or death forces us to attend.

Philip Yancey, Where Is God When It Hurts?

THE MAN IN THE GLASS

When you get what you want in your struggle
    for self
And the world makes you king for a day
Just go to the mirror and look at yourself
And see what that man has to say.
For it isn't your father, or mother, or wife

Whose judgment upon you must pass
The fellow whose verdict counts most in
    your life
Is the one staring back from the glass.
He's the fellow to please – never mind all
    the rest
For he's with you, clear to the end
And you've passed your most difficult,
    dangerous test
If the man in the glass is your friend.
You may fool the whole world down the
    pathway of years
And get pats on the back as you pass
But your final reward will be heartache and
    tears
If you've cheated the man in the glass.

Anon.

The second service that one should perform for another in a Christian community is that of active helpfulness. This means, initially, simple assistance in trifling, external matters. There is a multitude of these things wherever people live together. Nobody is too good for the meanest service. One who worries about the loss of time that such petty, outward acts of helpfulness entail is usually taking the importance of their own career too solemnly.

Dietrich Bonhoeffer

CHAPTER TEN

Sacrificial Love

✽ ✽ ✽

The dictionary definition of sacrifice is 'Slaughter of animal or person; surrender of a possession, as offering to deity; giving up of a thing for the sake of another that is higher or more urgent'.

The death of Christ on the cross at Calvary was the precious price God paid for our salvation. Jesus knew it was the way God's anger against our sin would be satisfied. He was prepared to pay the ultimate price – His life.

> He paid for you with the precious lifeblood
> of Christ, the sinless, spotless Lamb of God.
> God chose Him for this purpose long before
> the world began
>
> *1 Peter 1:18–19 (NLT)*

> How deep the Father's love for us,
> How vast beyond all measure,
> That He should give His only Son
> To make a wretch His treasure.
> How great the pain of searing loss,
> The Father turns His face away
> As wounds which mar the Chosen One
> Bring many sons to glory.

Behold the man upon a cross,
My sin upon His shoulders,
Ashamed I hear my mocking voice
Call out among the scoffers.
It was my sin that held Him there
Until it was accomplished,
His dying breath has brought me life
I know that it is finished.

I will not boast in anything,
No gifts, no power, no wisdom,
But I will boast in Jesus Christ,
His death and resurrection.
Why should I gain from His reward?
I cannot give an answer
But this I know with all my heart,
His wounds have paid my ransom.

Stuart Townend

'I am the good Shepherd ... and I lay down
my life for the sheep.'

John 10:14–15 (NIV)

I found this in a book written by Sir Cliff Richard many years ago and I have quoted it often as it describes in very simple terms the essence of God's love for us and Jesus' sacrifice. As he says, 'Jesus makes sense of it all'.

BUT SUPPOSE IT'S TRUE ...

Which kind of Christmas is yours? The one you have to struggle into, maybe like an old suit, somewhere early in December? The one that demands that you make an effort to be friendly, find time to send cards to people who might send them to you, and generally spend more money than normal to create the right impression? Inside there is the gnawing awareness that, come Twelfth Night when the cards and the Christmas tree are ditched, the play-acting will end and the real world will lurch back into focus. It's the motiveless Christmas. We send greetings, give presents, eat, drink and try to be merry because society says we should. It's December and that's how people in the West are expected to behave at that time of year.

The result is often destructive – a lot of people become acutely lonely, depressed and envious. The family next door is having a great time, so we reckon, but our circumstances are different.

If only contentment and fun could be switched on that easily. Of course they can't.

But there's the other Christmas – the real one – the one with the motive, the one that has Jesus in focus. I know you can't switch that on either. You can't make yourself believe Him or love Him – but can you understand that He makes sense of it all – the cards and the gifts, the parties and the daft hats? Just suppose for a moment that it really is true – that God really did love the world so much that He gave. It would revolutionise your Christmas – not to mention the rest of the year!

Someone once asked a Christian friend of mine, 'Supposing you're wrong about Christianity?' My friend replied, 'If I'm wrong, I'll have lost nothing and still had a fabulous life. But suppose you're wrong …?'

Cliff Richard

My Lord, what love is this,
That pays so dearly,
That I, the guilty one,
May go free!
Amazing love, O what sacrifice,
The Son of God, given for me.
My debt He pays,
And my death He dies,
That I might live.

And so, they watched Him die,
Despised, rejected;
But O, the blood He shed
Flowed for me.
Amazing love, O what sacrifice,
The Son of God, given for me.
My debt He pays,
And my death He dies,
That I might live.

And now, this love of Christ
Shall flow like rivers.
Come, wash your guilt away,
Live again.
Amazing love, O what sacrifice,
The Son of God, given for me.
My debt He pays,
And my death He dies,
That I might live.

Graham Kendrick

'I have loved you even as the Father has loved me. Remain in my love. When you obey me, you remain in my love, just as I obey my Father and remain in his love. I have told you this so that you will be filled with my joy. Yes, your joy will overflow! I command you to love each other in the same way that I love you. And here is how to measure it – the greatest love is shown when people lay down their lives for their friends. You are my friends if you obey me. I no longer call you servants, because a master doesn't confide in his servants. Now you are my friends, since I have told you everything the Father told me. You didn't choose me, I chose you. I appointed you to go and produce fruit that will last, so that the Father will give you whatever you ask for, using my Name. I command you to love each other.'

John 15:9–17 (NLT)

SALVATION'S COST

The story is told of a hero of the Chinese rice-fields during an earthquake. From his hilltop farm, he saw the ocean swiftly withdrawn, like some prodigious animal crouching for the leap, and knew the leap would be the tidal wave. He saw also that his neighbours working in low fields must be gathered to his hill or swept away. Without a second thought he set fire to his rice-ricks and furiously rang the temple bell. His neighbours thought his farm was on fire and rushed to help him. Then from the safe hill, they saw the swirl of waters over fields just forsaken – and knew their salvation and its cost.

Lafcadio Hearn

The greatest love of a man is his love for his friends; the greatest love of God is His love for His enemies; the highest Christian love is that a man will lay down his life for his Friend, the Lord Jesus Christ – 'I have called you friends'.

Oswald Chambers

Joni was a vivacious, pretty, young girl who, as the result of a diving accident, became a quadriplegic. Having come to terms with her situation she has served God powerfully from her wheelchair ever since. She is an eloquent speaker, singer and prolific writer.

A DELIBERATE HANDICAP

You probably know at least a few disabled people.

But did you ever think of Jesus in that category?

No, He didn't have a physical disability, but He did handicap Himself when He came to earth. Webster's Dictionary defines handicap as 'any difficulty which is imposed on a superior person so as to hamper or disadvantage him, making that person more equal with others.'

If we use that definition, then Jesus was handicapped. Think of it. On the one hand, He possessed the fullness of Almighty God, yet on the other hand He made Himself nothing. He emptied Himself, taking the very nature of a servant.

Talk about handicaps! To be God on the one hand ... yet to make Yourself nothing. What a severe limitation! You would think it must have hampered the Lord, put Him at a disadvantage.

Jesus, Master Architect of the universe, designed planets and stars, galaxies and nebulae, pulsars and quasars. On earth He was a carpenter, limiting Himself to stools and tables.

Jesus, the eternal Word, spoke time and space into being. On earth He chose to speak to prostitutes, lepers and sinners.

Jesus, the One who created the perfect bodies of Adam and Eve, despised pain and suffering as one of the awful results of the Fall. On earth, He endured backaches, cramped muscles, pangs of hunger and thirst. He sweated real sweat and cried real tears and bled real blood.

When I think of all this, it strikes me that these limitations didn't just 'happen' to Jesus in the same way circumstances 'happen' to you and me. The amazing thing is that Christ chose to be handicapped. I can't think of too many people who would make such a choice. I know I wouldn't.

But 'since the children have flesh and blood, He too shared in their humanity so that by His death He might destroy him who holds the power of death' (Heb. 2:14).

If you have a physical handicap, or maybe even an emotional or mental one, then you're not in bad company. If anything, you're in an elite fellowship with Christ Himself.

We had no choice over our handicap.

He did, and chose to be limited … so that He might set us free.

Joni Eareckson Tada, God's Glorious Intruder

A missionary friend of my daughter's in Lima, Peru, was explaining to an elderly shanty-town dweller, in his little shack, that it was so cold in England at the time, and the snow was so thick, that the milkman couldn't get around to deliver the milk.

He answered, 'Those poor people in England can't get their milk and here I am with everything I need!' Humbling words!

> A man's life consisteth not in the abundance
> of the things which he possesseth.
>
> *Luke 12:15 (AV)*

> Whate'er God does is well,
> Whether He gives or takes,
> And what we from His hand receive
> Suffices us to live.
> He takes, and gives, while yet He loves us still.
> Then love His will.
>
> *B. Schmolck*

For myself, I am certain that the good of human life cannot lie in the possession of things which for one man to possess is for the rest to lose, but rather in things which all can possess alike, where one man's wealth promotes his neighbour's.

Spinoza

Every lot is happy to a person who bears it with tranquillity.

Boethius

This is part of the introduction to Carole Mayhall's book, Words that Hurt, Words that Heal. *It never fails to move me when I realise how easily we can take God's precious Word for granted.*

Six hundred women swarmed into the hive-shaped banquet hall and fluttered to rest. The buzzing became a low hum and finally stilled as we waited for the evening session of the conference to begin.

Dennis was an eloquent speaker, and challenged us with story after story of taking the Bible to East Asia. His climaxing illustration left me shaken.

On a recent visit to an Asian church, he sat next to a small woman whose hands were so crippled she could not hold the hymnbook. Following the service, he turned to her and asked, 'Do you have a Bible?'

'No,' she said softly.

'Would you like to have one?' he queried.

'Oh, yes!' Her face brightened.

'If you will come back to my hotel, I will give you one,' offered Dennis.

As they walked back to his hotel, Dennis asked the diminutive woman about her hands. She told him the following story.

'When the soldiers were searching for all Bibles, hymnbooks and religious material, they came to my door. I had hidden my Bible under the cold ashes of my stove, but they knew all the places to look. As they were taking my Bible from my house, I grabbed it and said, "Oh, please don't take my Bible. It's all that I have to tell me about my Jesus."

'The men said, "It's nothing but a book of fables. Give it to us, old woman."

'But again I cried, "Oh, please don't take it. It's all that I have that tells me about my Jesus."'

The woman said they took her outside, stripped her, and put her up on a platform to shame her before the crowds. For four hours she sat with the Bible clutched to her naked breast, head down as the crowds mocked and spit on her. They thought she was ashamed, but she was praying.

She continued, 'After four hours they again tried to take my Bible but I clung to it and said, "Please don't take it. It's all I have that tells me about my Jesus."'

Angrily they spread her out in the dirt with her hands stretched over her head and beat her hands with a hammer until they were nothing but pulp. To this day she cannot even feed herself.

As I listened to this story, I was deeply touched. Dennis was totally committed to taking the Word of God to dangerous places. The woman was totally committed to Christ and to His Word.

Carole Mayhall

THE FINAL JUDGMENT

'But when the Son of Man comes in his glory, and all the angels with him, then he will sit upon his glorious throne. All the nations will be gathered in his presence, and he will separate them as a shepherd separates the sheep from the goats. He will place the sheep at his right hand and the goats at his left. Then the King will say to those on the right, "Come you who are blessed by my Father, inherit the kingdom prepared for you before the foundation of the world. For I was hungry, and you fed me, I was thirsty, and you gave me a drink. I was a stranger and you invited me into your home. I was naked and you gave me clothing. I was sick and you cared for me. I was in prison, and you visited me."

'Then the righteous ones will reply, "Lord, when did we ever see you hungry and feed you? Or thirsty and give you something to drink? Or a stranger and show you hospitality? Or naked and give you clothing? When did we ever see you sick or in prison, and visit you?" And the King will tell them, "I assure you, when you did it to one of the least of these my brothers and sisters, you were doing it to me!"

'Then the King will turn to those on the left and say, "Away with you, you cursed ones, into the eternal fire prepared for the Devil and his demons! For I was hungry, and you didn't feed me. I was thirsty, and you didn't give me anything to drink. I was a stranger, and you didn't invite me into your home. I was naked, and you gave me no clothing. I was sick and in prison, and you didn't visit me."

'Then they will reply, "Lord, when did we ever see you hungry or thirsty or a stranger or naked or sick or in prison, and not help you?" And he will answer, "I assure you, when you refused to help the least of these my brothers and sisters, you were refusing to help me." And they will go away into eternal punishment, but the righteous will go into eternal life.'

Matthew 25:31-46 (NLT)

People say to me: why do you go on remembering the Holocaust? It's over, finished, it happened a long time ago. Forgive and forget. My answer is simple. We remember, not for the sake of the past but for the sake of the future. We remember so that when we see again people driven from their homes, deprived of rights, dispossessed and crying for help, we don't sit still and do nothing. Those who forget the past are destined to repeat it. And there are certain things we just can't let happen again.'

As we approach the end of this, the bloodiest century in history, we have reached a crossroad in the human journey. The sheer scale of our technology has given us the most powerful double-edged weapon ever held by human hands. We can use it to build or destroy; to kill or to heal; to create suffering or justice. It depends on us, each one of us; what we cherish, what we remember, what we're prepared to fight for, our passion for justice.

Jonathan Sachs, Chief Rabbi

> Speak up for those who cannot speak for
> themselves; ensure justice for those who are
> perishing. Yes, speak up for the poor and
> helpless, and see that they get justice.

Proverbs 31:8–9 (NLT)

Another woman, also serving on the front
lines, captures for me in a single image all
the elements of the skin of Christ's Body. I
visited a nun, Dr Pfau, in the 1950's outside
Karachi, Pakistan, in the worst human
squalor I have ever encountered. Long
before I reached the place, a putrid smell
burned my nostrils. It was a smell you could
almost lean on.

Soon I could see an immense garbage
dump by the sea, the accumulated refuse of a
large city that had been stagnating and
rotting for several months. The air was
humming with flies. As last I could make out
human figures – people covered with sores –
crawling over the mounds of garbage. They
had leprosy, and more than a hundred of
them banished from Karachi, had set up
home in this dump. Sheets of corrugated
iron marked off the shelters, and a single
dripping tap in the centre of the dump
provided their only source of water.

But there, beside this awful place, I saw a

neat wooden clinic in which I found Dr Pfau. She proudly showed me her orderly shelves and files of beautifully kept records on each patient in the dump. The stark contrast between the horrible scene outside and the oasis of love and concern inside her tidy clinic burned deep into my mind. Dr Pfau was daily exhibiting all the properties of skin: beauty, sensitivity to needs, compliancy, and the steady, fearless application of divine love through human touch. All over the world people like her are fulfilling Christ's command to fill the earth with His presence.

Philip Yancey, Where Is God When It Hurts?

I love the story I heard about a little boy who was walking along a shore and suddenly saw thousands of starfish washed up on the beach. Realising they would die out of the water, he started systematically throwing them back into the sea, one by one. A man came along and started ridiculing him, saying with so many starfish washed up, he would never get them all back in that water and really couldn't make much difference if he worked all day. The little boy paused, then picked up another starfish and, as he threw it back into the water, said, 'I've made a difference for that one.'

'And if you give even a cup of water to one of the least of my followers, you will surely be rewarded.'

Matthew10:42 (NLT)

Though he was God he did not demand and cling to his rights as God. He made himself nothing; he took the humble position of a slave and appeared in human form. And in human form he obediently humbled himself even further by dying a criminal's death on a cross.

Philippians 2:6–8 (NLT)

Empty your cup for others and it will always be full. Break yourself open for others and you will become whole.

Lloyd Ogilvie

PATIENCE

You suffered throughout your life, O Lord Jesus Christ, that I might be saved. And yet, even now, You continue to bear with me, as I constantly stumble upon the path and go astray. As often as I become impatient and wish to abandon Your way, You encourage me, and stretch forth Your helping hand. Each day I increase Your burden; yet while I am impatient, Your patience is infinite.

Søren Kierkegaard

A sailor on the south coast of England told his chaplain, 'Chaplain, you don't understand. You're telling us to walk the straight and narrow path. But you don't realise the temptations we face, the way we're blown and tossed about. We can't really be blamed for what happens to us.'

The chaplain drew the sailor's attention to the water, where two sailboats were moving along with their sails flapping in the wind. One was heading west, the other east. The chaplain said, 'One boat goes east, one boat goes west. By the self-same winds that blow. It's the set of the sails, and not the gales that determine which way they will go.'

Do we have our sails set in the direction of obedience to God? If so, we can go the right way, even if the whole world is blown off course.

Alistair Begg, The Hand of God

To have, each day, the thing I wish,
Lord, that seems best to me;
But not to have the thing I wish,
Lord, that seems best to Thee.
Most truly then, Thy will be done
When mine, O Lord, is crossed,
'Tis good to see my plans o'erthrown
My ways in Thine all lost.

Horatius Bonar

O, Lord, Thou knowest what is best for us;
let this or that be done, as Thou shalt please.
Give what Thou wilt, and how much Thou
wilt, and when Thou wilt. Deal with me as
Thou thinkest good. Set me where Thou
wilt, and deal with me in all things just as
Thou wilt. Behold, I am Thy servant,
prepared for all things; for I desire not to live
unto myself, but unto Thee; and oh, that I
could do it worthily and perfectly!

Thomas à Kempis

Now, no one is likely to die for a good person, though someone might be willing to die for a person who is especially good. But God showed his love for us by sending Christ to die for us while we were still sinners.

Romans 5:7–8 (NLT)

The following story is an excerpt from a powerful and moving book, Miracle on the River Kwai, *by Ernest Gordon, which speaks of his time as a prisoner of war, building the Railroad of Death.*

LEST WE FORGET …

Stories began to circulate around the camp, stories of self-sacrifice, heroism, faith and love.

'Do you remember Angus McGillivray?' Dusty Miller asked me late one afternoon as he prepared me for my wash.

'Indeed I do,' I replied. 'He was in my company. A darned good soldier, too. I know him well. As a matter of fact, I defended him at a court martial on the charge of refusing to obey an order given him by his platoon sergeant. In my opinion he had every right to do so. It was a stupid order. But when Angus queried it he was immediately put under arrest.'

Dusty waited with interest as I continued my recollections.

'At the trial I put everything I had into the defence. Pulled out every stop in the organ. Backed every fact with reams of law; I'd studied law while I was in the army. I was doing so well that at the end of the first day Angus MacDonald, the adjutant who was prosecuting said to me, "You've won hands down. I'm on McGillivray's side now."'

'Did you get an acquittal?'

'No. The court acquitted him of the charge of disobeying an order, but got him on the nebulous charge of "Conduct prejudicial to good order and military discipline". I've always thought it was damned bad law to have a charge as general as that on the books. Every soldier worth his salt could be convicted of it at some time or another. The adjutant admitted that it was the sergeant who should have been convicted and not Angus McGillivray. Aye, Angus was a good soldier all right. He came from Lochgilphead at the head of Loch Fyne. Fine stock in his family.'

'Was he in the battalion long?' Dusty asked.

'For the length of his service, which must have been over eight years. He was on the northwest frontier of India most of the time the battalion was fighting there. But why were you asking me if I knew him?'

'He's dead.'

'Dead? How?'

For a moment Dusty could not speak. I could see that he was deeply moved. I wondered why, for he could scarcely have known MacGillivray.

'It's hard to say. He was strong. In fact, he was one of those you'd expect would be the last to die. But then I suppose he needn't have died.'

'Then why did he?'

Dusty sat down on my bed. 'It has to do with Angus's mucker,' he began, 'who became very ill.'

It was the custom among the Argylls for every man to have a 'mucker' – that is, a pal or friend with whom he shared or 'mucked in' everything he had.

'It seemed pretty certain to everyone,' Dusty continued, 'that the mucker was going to die. Certain, that is, to everyone but Angus. He made up his mind that his mucker would live. Someone had stolen his mucker's blanket. Angus gave him his own. Every mealtime Angus would show up to draw his ration. But he didn't eat it. He would bring it round to give to his friend. Stood over him, he did, and made him eat it. Going hungry was hard on Angus, mind you, because he was a big man with a big frame.'

As Dusty talked on, I could see it all happening – Angus drawing on his strength through his will and depleting his own body to make his friend live.

'His mates noticed that Angus had taken to slipping out of the camp at night.' Dusty went on. 'These excursions could only have one purpose. He was visiting the Thai villages. It was taken for granted that he had joined the black marketeers! Angus, of all people! This shocked the others for he was known as a man of high principles.'

As men died in the camp, it became possible for others to come into possession of objects of some value – watches, shirts, shorts, knives and so on. These were highly prized by the Thais, who would gladly pay for them in their paper money known as 'bahts' worth about one and sixpence each. Or they would barter for the goods, offering medicine or duck eggs.

'Although Angus's mates thought he was trying to make a bit of money for himself, they didn't begrudge it to him,' said Dusty. 'Perhaps you can guess the end of the story. The mucker got better. Then Angus collapsed. Just pitched on his face and died.'

'And what did the docs say caused it?' I asked.

'Starvation,' answered Dusty, 'complicated by exhaustion.'

Dusty sat in stillness.

After a while I said, 'Do you remember that verse from St John that used to be read at memorial services for those who died in the First World War? It went like this: "Greater love hath no man ..."'

'Yes, I remember it,' said Dusty, nodding. 'I've always thought it was one of the most beautiful passages in the New Testament. "This is My commandment, that ye love one another as I have loved you. Greater love hath no man than this, that a man lay down his life for his friends."'

Dusty stood without moving. Then he said, 'That's Angus all right.'

'By some ways of reckoning,' I said, 'what he did might seem foolish.'

'But in other ways,' Dusty returned, 'it makes an awful lot of sense.'

He bent over my legs and began cleaning my ulcers.

During the next few days, on my visits to the latrine, I heard other prisoners discussing Angus's sacrifice. The story of what he had done was spreading through the camp. It had evidently fired the imagination of everyone. He had given us a shining example of the way we ought to live, even if we did not.

Yet, noble as Angus's sacrifice was, it was not the only one. Other incidents were now spoken of, that showed that death no longer had the last word at Chungkai. One that went the rounds soon after concerned another Argyll, who was in a work detail on the railway.

The day's works had ended; the tools were being counted, as usual. As the party was about to be dismissed, the Japanese guard shouted that a shovel was missing. He insisted that someone had stolen it to sell to the Thais. Striding up and down before the men, he ranted and denounced them, for their wickedness, and most unforgivable of all their ingratitude to the Emperor.

As he raved, he worked himself up into a paranoid fury. Screaming in broken English, he demanded that the guilty one step forward to take his punishment. No one moved; the guard's rage reached new heights of violence. 'All die! All die!' he shrieked.

To show that he meant what he said he cocked his rifle, put it to his shoulder and looked down the sights, ready to fire at the first man at the end of them.

At that moment, the Argyll stepped forward, stood stiffly to attention and said, 'I did it.'

The guard unleashed all his whipped-up hate; he kicked the helpless prisoner and beat him with his fists. Still the Argyll stood rigidly to attention, with the blood streaming down his face. His silence goaded the guard to an excess of rage. Seizing his rifle by the barrel, he lifted it high over his head and, with a final howl, brought it down on the skull of the Argyll, who sank limply to the ground and did not move. Although it was perfectly clear he was dead, that guard continued to beat him and stopped only when exhausted.

The men of the work detail picked up their comrade's body, shouldered their tools and marched back to camp. When the tools were counted again, at the guardhouse, no shovel was missing.

As this story was told, remarkably enough, admiration for the Argyll transcended hatred for the guard.

News of similar happenings began to reach our ears from other camps. One incident concerned an Aussie private who had been caught outside the fence while trying to obtain medicine from the Thais for his sick friends. He was summarily tried and sentenced to death.

On the morning set for his execution, he marched cheerfully between his guards to the parade ground. The Japanese were out in full force to observe the scene. The Aussie was permitted to have his commanding offer and a chaplain in attendance as witnesses. The party came to a halt. The C.O. and the chaplain were waved to one side, and the Aussie was left standing alone. Calmly, he surveyed his executioners. He knelt down and drew a small New Testament from a pocket in his ragged shorts. Unhurriedly, his lips moving but no sound coming from them, he read a passage to himself.

What that passage was, no one will ever know. I cannot help wondering, however, if it were not those words addressed by Jesus to His disciples in the Upper Room:

Let not your heart be troubled; ye believe in God, believe also in Me.

In My Father's house are many mansions; if it were not so, I would have told you. I go to prepare a place for you.

And if I go and prepare a place for you I will come again and receive you to Myself; That where I am, ye may be also.

... Peace I leave with you, my peace I give unto you; not as the world giveth, give I unto you. let not your heart be troubled; neither let it be afraid.

He finished reading, returned his New Testament to his pocket, looked up, and saw the distressed face of his chaplain. He smiled, waved to him, and called out, 'Cheer up, Padre, it isn't as bad as all that. I'll be all right.'

He nodded to his executioner as a sign that he was ready. He knelt down, and bent his head to expose his neck.

The Samurai sword flashed in the sunlight.

Ernest Gordon, Miracle on the River Kwai

The love of Jesus that grew in these men's hearts caused a total transformation of their prisoner of war camp.

And in conclusion …

Lord, for the years your love has kept and guided,
  urged and inspired us, cheered us on our way,
sought us and saved us, pardoned and provided,
  Lord of the years, we bring our thanks today.

Lord, for that word, the word of life which fires us,
  speaks to our hearts and sets our souls ablaze,
teaches and trains, rebukes us and inspires us;
  Lord of the word, receive your people's praise.

Lord, for our land, in this our generation,
  spirits oppressed by pleasure, wealth and care;
for young and old, for commonwealth and nation,
  Lord of our land, be pleased to hear our prayer.

Lord, for our world; when we disown and doubt
  him,
  loveless in strength, and comfortless in pain;
hungry and helpless, lost indeed without him,
  Lord of the world, we pray that Christ may reign.

Lord, for ourselves; in living power remake us,
  self on the cross and Christ upon the throne;
past put behind us, for the future take us,
  Lord of our lives, to live for Christ alone.

Timothy Dudley-Smith

But Lord, Your landmark is love.
More vulnerable than any tower.
Weaker, yet stronger, than any stone.
Enduring, when all else fails.
Invisible,
Yet clear to see with eyes of faith.
Shape me, Lord,
As the mason shapes his stone,
With firm blows lovingly aimed,
That I may take my place,
A living stone in Your temple.

Lord, I base my life
On the compass point of Your love.
Lead me to it
Whatever road I take.
And help me point others to it,
By all I do and say.

Eddie Askew, Disguises of Love

And now, dear brothers and sisters, let me say one more thing as I close this letter. Fix your thoughts on what is true and honourable and right. Think about things that are pure and lovely and admirable. Think about things that are excellent and worthy of praise. Keep putting into practice all you learned from me and heard from me and saw me doing, and the God of peace will be with you.

Philippians 4:8–9 (NLT)

Index of First Lines, Titles and Authors

❋ ❋ ❋

forgiveness   — mercy
joy   —

learn { humility   in God's love — service   —
show { strength   — justice / equality
                                        Remem

p.74 — not in ripture — our bend down — "humility"